pocket PIES

MINI EMPANADAS, PASTIES, TURNOVERS & MORE

pocket *PIES*

MINI EMPANADAS, PASTIES, TURNOVERS & MORE

PAMELA CLARK

STERLING
New York

Contents

pastry   6

poultry pies   10

meat pies   28

vegetable pies   80

seafood pies   104

sweet pies & tarts   120

index   156

The oven temperatures in this book are for conventional ovens; if you have a convection oven, decrease the temperature by 10-20 degrees.

pastry

Pastry is one of those things in the culinary world that is well worth mastering – especially the ever-popular shortcrust pastry, be it sweet or savory. Frozen sheets of various types of pastry, including sweet and savory shortcrust, are readily available in supermarkets, and no home freezer should be without them for those last-minute tops for pies, turnovers and pasties. Goodies made using pastry are usually eaten in the cooler months; ideally, pastry should always be made in a cool kitchen. Allow yourself time to make pastry; it's well worth it.

Like everything else, particularly in the baking area, there are some rules involved. Use a good basic recipe like the one opposite, and follow the recipe and the rules very carefully.

Perfect pastry has a "look" and a "feel" to it – it should be easy to handle and easy to roll without major cracks. Try to remember the way it looked and felt, then aim to come up with that same result every time; it's a good idea to make notes to yourself on the recipe.

Cool fingertips with a light touch make good pastry; hot hands and heavy handling don't. Food processors make good pastry too, providing the ingredients are "pulsed" together using short bursts of power; process only until the ingredients cling together.

Over-handling or over-processing will result in tough, hard-to-roll pastry; it will develop large cracks during the rolling process.

basic shortcrust pastry

1½ cups plain (all-purpose) flour
4 ounces cold butter, chopped coarsely
1 egg yolk
2 tablespoons iced water, approximately

HAND-MADE METHOD
Sift flour into large bowl, rub in butter with fingertips. Add egg yolk and enough of the water to make ingredients barely cling together. Knead pastry lightly on floured surface until smooth; press into a circle shape. Enclose pastry in plastic wrap, refrigerate 30 minutes.

PROCESSOR METHOD
Sift flour into processor bowl, add butter, pulse until mixture is crumbly. Add egg yolk and most of the water, pulse until ingredients barely cling together, add more water if necessary. Knead pastry lightly on floured surface until smooth; press into circle shape. Enclose pastry in plastic wrap, refrigerate 30 minutes.

Sweet shortcrust pastry variation: Sift 2 tablespoons confectioners' sugar with the flour.
Note: This recipe makes the equivalent of two sheets of store-bought shortcrust pastry.

About the ingredients:

All the ingredients, and even the mixing bowl, should be chilled.

Flour

Weigh or measure the flour, add a pinch of salt if you like, sift it into a mixing bowl – or the bowl of a food processor – then refrigerate it for about 30 minutes. Confectioner's sugar: Add it to the sifter with the flour (and salt) for sweet shortcrust pastry.

Butter

The butter must be very cold, even partly frozen. Chop it into ½ inch cubes, or, if it's hard and cold enough, coarsely grate it, then place it into either the mixing or food processor bowl.

Rub the butter through the flour using fingertips, or pulse the processor until the butter is evenly distributed through the flour. The mixture should be slightly coarse, not too fine, or the butter and flour will come together before any liquid is added.

Egg yolk, lemon juice, water

Usually one or two of these ingredients is used to bind the flour and butter mixture together. The secret to making perfect pastry is knowing just how much of these ingredients to add; this knowledge comes with experience.

Insufficient liquid will result in a pastry that is crumbly and almost impossible to roll out; it will develop large cracks during the rolling process. Too much liquid will make the pastry too soft and sticky and the pastry will shrink during baking. Most recipes will suggest an approximate amount of liquid; it's a judgment call and each time pastry is made the amount of liquid needed will vary slightly. This is due to the rate at which the flour absorbs the liquid: old flour (more dehydrated) will absorb more liquid than new (less dehydrated) flour.

The liquid should be added as fast as possible – that is, preferably in one batch, not in small amounts. Once again, over-handling or over-processing will result in tough pastry. Practice makes (for) perfect (pastry).

step-by-step

Cool ingredients, cool fingertips and a light touch are the keys to perfect pastry.

Kneading pastry

Strictly speaking, pastry isn't really kneaded as a bread dough would be kneaded; it's just quickly and lightly shaped into a block or circle for the resting process.

Use the least amount of flour possible when shaping the pastry, just enough to stop the dough sticking to the counter or board.

Marble is the perfect surface on which to handle pastry, and stainless steel is quite good too, but a laminated, tiled or timber surface works well enough.

Resting pastry

The resting time in the refrigerator for pastry is usually about 30 minutes – this is vital for success. During this time, the protein (gluten) in the flour relaxes, resulting in pastry that feels great in the mouth.

Resting is usually done right after the pastry is made. Shape the pastry into a block or circle, the same thickness all the way through, enclose the pastry in plastic wrap and refrigerate for the time stated in the recipe. A lot of recipes suggest another resting after the pastry has been rolled out and the dish lined (the ideal time is usually 20 to 30 minutes). Some recipes suggest freezing the pastry for the last resting.

Once again this resting allows the now-slightly-stretched pastry – due to the rolling-out process – time to relax; it also helps to minimize shrinkage during the baking process.

Rolling pastry

This is done either on the counter, using a minimum amount of flour to prevent sticking – excess flour simply upsets the balance of the ingredients – or between sheets of parchment or greaseproof paper.

There are many types, sizes and shapes of rolling pins available, made from wood, ceramic, plastic or glass; all work well. It's important when pastry is being rolled out that an even pressure is used to try and keep the pastry the same thickness all the way through.

Roll in short light strokes from the center out to the edge of the pastry; never roll over the edge of the pastry or it may become too thin and difficult to lift off the paper.

Lining a dish or pan

If the pastry has been rolled out on the counter, place the rolling pin in the center of the pastry, flap half the pastry over the pin, hold the pin up with one hand, supporting the pastry underneath with the other hand.

Lift the pastry over the dish and ease it over the base, remove the pin, then gently push the pastry around the side of the dish, without stretching it. If the pastry has been rolled between sheets of parchment paper, remove the top layer of paper, support the pastry underneath the remaining paper, then turn the pastry into the dish. Peel the paper away and ease the pastry around the side of the dish.

Trim the edge of the pastry by rolling the pin over the dish.

Docking pastry

Some recipes require the pastry to be "docked" to prevent it rising. Prick the pastry all over, about ¾ inch apart, using a fork or a pastry docker. If the pastry case is in a dish with a deep side like a pie dish, prick the side or wall of the pastry as well as the base.

Baking blind

Sometimes it is necessary to bake the pastry blind (i.e., cook it without a filling). For best results, follow individual recipes. Line the uncooked pastry case with either a piece of foil or parchment paper, fill the cavity with uncooked rice, pulses or ceramic or metal beads. This is to weight the pastry evenly to prevent rising during the baking. Bake the pastry case for the specified time. Remove the dish from the oven, carefully lift the foil or paper up to remove the weights from the pastry case to the counter. Leave the weights to cool completely before sealing in an airtight container for future use; don't use for cooking. Return the pastry case to the oven for further baking. Usually the whole baking blind process takes between 15 and 20 minutes.

poultry pies

chinese duck & five-spice pies

4-pound whole duck
1 tablespoon vegetable oil
4 shallots, chopped finely
2 tablespoons plain (all-purpose) flour
½ cup chicken stock
¼ cup chinese cooking wine
2 tablespoons light soy sauce
2 tablespoons orange juice
2 teaspoons light brown sugar
4 cinnamon sticks
1 egg, beaten lightly

FIVE-SPICE PASTRY
2 cups plain (all-purpose) flour
2 teaspoons finely grated orange rind
½ teaspoon five-spice powder
4 ounces butter, chopped coarsely
1 egg
1 tablespoon water

1 Rinse duck under cold water. Place duck in large saucepan; cover with cold water. Bring to a boil, uncovered, reduce heat; simmer, covered, 30 minutes. Cool in water in pan. Remove meat from duck; discard skin and bones. Shred meat.
2 Meanwhile, make five-spice pastry.
3 Heat oil in large frying pan; cook shallot, stirring, until soft. Add flour; cook, stirring, 1 minute. Gradually stir in combined stock, wine, sauce, juice and sugar; bring to a boil. Simmer, uncovered, 3 minutes. Add duck; season to taste. Cool.
4 Preheat oven to 400°F. Grease four (1-cup) round pie pans. Roll pastry between sheets of parchment paper until large enough to line pans with 2 inches of pastry overhanging. Lift pastry into pans, press into base and side. Divide duck mixture among pies. Fold excess pastry over filling to enclose. Position a cinnamon stick on each pie; brush with egg.
5 Bake about 25 minutes. Stand pies in pans for 5 minutes before serving.

FIVE-SPICE PASTRY Process flour, rind and five-spice until combined. Add butter; process until crumbly. Add egg and water; process until ingredients just come together. Knead dough on floured surface until smooth. Enclose in plastic wrap; refrigerate 30 minutes.

prep + cook time 1 hour 30 minutes (+ cooling & refrigeration) makes 4
nutritional count per serving 139.2g total fat (50.7g saturated fat); 1730 cal; 66.5g carbohydrate; 51g protein; 3.4g fiber

chicken, mushroom & tarragon pies

1½ ounces butter
6½ ounces button mushrooms, sliced
1½ pounds boneless chicken thighs, chopped coarsely
1 tablespoon plain (all-purpose) flour
¾ cup chicken stock
1 tablespoon finely chopped fresh tarragon
1 egg, beaten lightly

TARRAGON PASTRY
1½ cups plain (all-purpose) flour
¼ cup finely grated parmesan cheese
2 tablespoons finely chopped fresh tarragon
4 ounces butter, chopped coarsely
1 egg
1 tablespoon iced water, approximately

1 Make tarragon pastry.
2 Melt butter in large frying pan; cook mushrooms, stirring, until browned. Add chicken; cook, stirring, until browned. Add flour; cook, stirring, 1 minute. Gradually stir in stock; stir over heat until mixture boils and thickens. Season; cool. Stir in tarragon.
3 Preheat oven to 400°F. Oil four (1-cup) metal pie pans. Divide pastry in half. Roll one half between sheets of parchment paper until large enough to line pans. Cut pastry into four squares, lift into pans, press into base and sides; trim edges.
4 Divide chicken mixture among pies. Roll remaining pastry between sheets of parchment paper. Cut four 5½-inch rounds from pastry; place over chicken mixture. Press edges to seal. Refrigerate 20 minutes. Brush tops with egg; cut a slit in pies. Bake about 30 minutes. Stand in pans 5 minutes.

TARRAGON PASTRY Process flour, cheese, tarragon and butter until crumbly. Add egg and enough of the water to make ingredients just come together. Knead dough on floured surface until smooth. Cover; refrigerate 30 minutes.

prep + cook time 1 hour 10 minutes (+ refrigeration & cooling) **makes** 4
nutritional count per serving 52.6g total fat (28.4g saturated fat); 845 cal; 43.9g carbohydrate; 48.9g protein; 3.5g fiber

chicken, fennel and celery pie

1 tablespoon olive oil
1 medium fennel bulb, trimmed, sliced thinly
2 celery sticks, trimmed, chopped coarsely
1 medium leek, chopped coarsely
1½ pounds boneless chicken breast, chopped coarsely
1 clove garlic, crushed
2 tablespoons plain (all-purpose) flour
1 cup chicken stock
½ cup light cream
1 egg white

SOUR CREAM PASTRY
1½ cups plain (all-purpose) flour
2½ ounces cold butter, chopped
⅓ cup sour cream
1 egg yolk

1 Make sour cream pastry.
2 Meanwhile, heat oil in large saucepan, cook fennel, celery and leek until softened. Add chicken and garlic; cook, stirring, until chicken changes color. Add flour; cook, stirring, until mixture thickens and bubbles. Gradually add combined stock and cream; stir until mixture boils and thickens. Reduce heat, simmer, uncovered, about 10 minutes or until thickened; season. Transfer to 6-cup ovenproof dish. Cool 20 minutes.
3 Preheat oven to 400°F.
4 Roll pastry between sheets of parchment paper until large enough to cover dish. Cover dish with pastry, trim edges. Seal edges with fork; use pastry scraps to decorate pie. Brush with egg white. Bake about 45 minutes or until browned.

SOUR CREAM PASTRY Process flour and butter until crumbly. Add cream and yolk, process until mixture comes together. Knead pastry on floured surface until smooth, cover; refrigerate 30 minutes.

prep + cook time 1 hour 30 minutes (+ cooling)
serves 4
nutritional count per serving 47.4g total fat (27g saturated fat); 811 cal; 49g carbohydrate; 45.1g protein; 5.8g fiber

note Sour cream pastry is lighter in texture but richer in flavor than basic shortcrust pastry. It is extremely easy to handle and may be used for both savory and sweet pies.

gooey chicken, brie and cranberry pies

2 teaspoons olive oil
6½ ounces chicken tenderloins
2 sheets shortcrust pastry
⅓ cup cranberry sauce
¾ ounce baby spinach leaves
3 ounces brie cheese, sliced thinly
1 egg, beaten lightly

1 Preheat oven to 425°F. Line oven tray with parchment paper.
2 Heat oil in medium frying pan; season chicken. Cook chicken until browned and cooked through. Remove from pan; slice thinly. Cool.

3 Cut four 4-inch rounds from one sheet of pastry. Place rounds on tray. Spread with sauce, leaving ½-inch border. Top with spinach, chicken and cheese. Cut four 4½-inch rounds from remaining pastry sheet. Cover filling; press pastry edges with a fork to seal.
4 Brush pastries with egg. Cut a small slit in center of each pie. Bake about 20 minutes or until browned lightly.

prep + cook time 35 minutes (+ cooling) **makes** 4
nutritional count per serving 34.6g total fat (17.7g saturated fat); 590 cal; 46.9g carbohydrate; 23.1g protein; 1.7g fiber

serving suggestion Serve with salad.

butter chicken puffs

¾ ounce butter
1 small yellow onion, chopped finely
8 ounces ground chicken
1 small carrot, grated coarsely
2 tablespoons butter chicken curry paste
2 tablespoons frozen peas
3 sheets puff pastry
1 egg, beaten lightly

1 Preheat oven to 425°F. Line oven tray with parchment paper.
2 Melt butter in large frying pan; cook onion, stirring, until soft. Add chicken; cook, stirring, until browned. Add carrot, paste and peas; cook for 5 minutes.
3 Cut four 4½-inch rounds from each pastry sheet. Place rounded tablespoons of mixture on one side of rounds. Fold over to form a semi-circle. Press edges together to seal; place on tray. Brush with egg; cut three slits in each puff.
4 Bake about 20 minutes or until browned.

prep + cook time 40 minutes **makes** 12
nutritional count per serving 14g total fat (2.3g saturated fat); 222 cal; 16.2g carbohydrate; 7.3g protein; 1.2g fiber

serving suggestion Serve with a yogurt and mint dipping sauce.

thai chicken curry pies

2 tablespoons peanut oil
1 medium yellow onion, sliced thinly
1 clove garlic, crushed
4-inch stick fresh lemon grass, chopped finely
¾-inch piece fresh ginger, grated
1½ pounds boneless chicken thighs,
    cut into 1¼-in pieces
1 teaspoon ground cumin
½ teaspoon ground turmeric
5¼ ounce can coconut milk
1 tablespoon cornstarch
¼ cup chicken stock
1 tablespoon fish sauce
1 fresh kaffir lime leaf, shredded finely
1 fresh long red chili, sliced thinly
¼ cup coarsely chopped fresh cilantro
2 sheets ready-rolled shortcrust pastry
1 egg, beaten lightly
2 sheets ready-rolled puff pastry

1 Heat oil in large saucepan; cook onion, garlic, lemon grass and ginger, stirring, until onion softens. Add chicken; cook, stirring, until browned. Add spices; cook, stirring, until fragrant. Add coconut milk; bring to a boil. Reduce heat; simmer, uncovered, 10 minutes. Add cornstarch and stock; cook, stirring, until mixture boils and thickens; cool. Stir in sauce, lime leaf, chili and cilantro.
2 Preheat oven to 400°F. Grease six-hole (¾ cup) texas muffin pan.
3 Cut six 4½-inch rounds from shortcrust pastry; press into pan holes. Brush edges with a little of the egg. Divide chicken curry among pastry cases.
4 Cut six 3½-inch rounds from puff pastry; top chicken mixture with puff pastry rounds. Press edges firmly to seal. Brush tops with remaining egg. Cut a small slit in top of each pie.
5 Bake about 25 minutes. Stand pies in pan 5 minutes before serving, top-side up.

prep + cook time 75 minutes (+ cooling) **serves** 6
nutritional count per pie 45.4g total fat
(21.4g saturated fat); 719 cal; 49.6g carbohydrate;
27.7g protein; 2.3g fiber

country chicken and vegetable pie

  2 tablespoons olive oil
  1 pound boneless chicken breasts,
     chopped coarsely
  1 medium yellow onion, chopped coarsely
  1 large carrot, chopped coarsely
  1 celery stalk, trimmed, chopped coarsely
5½ ounces button mushrooms, sliced thickly
  2 medium potatoes, chopped coarsely
  1 tablespoon plain (all-purpose) flour
 ½ cup dry white wine
  1 cup chicken stock
 ⅓ cup light cream
 ½ cup frozen peas
  2 tablespoons coarsely chopped fresh
     flat-leaf parsley
  1 sheet puff pastry
  1 egg, beaten lightly

1 Preheat oven to 425°F. Oil 6-cup ovenproof dish.
2 Heat half the oil in large saucepan; cook chicken until browned lightly all over. Remove from pan.
3 Heat remaining oil in same pan; cook onion, carrot, celery and mushrooms, stirring, until vegetables soften. Add potato, cook for 1 minute. Add flour; cook, stirring, until mixture bubbles and thickens. Gradually stir in wine, boil, stirring, 1 minute. Return chicken to pan with stock; bring to the boil. Simmer, uncovered, about 8 minutes until potato is tender. Stir in cream, peas and parsley; season to taste. Cool.
4 Spoon mixture into dish. Top with pastry. Trim edge; brush with egg. Bake pie about 20 minutes.

prep + cook time 50 minutes (+ cooling) **serves** 4
nutritional count per serving 29.9g total fat (8g saturated fat); 584 cal; 33.2g carbohydrate; 38.2g protein; 4.7g fiber

17

vietnamese chicken wonton cups

18 wonton wrappers
cooking-oil spray
  2 cups shredded barbecued chicken
  1 small carrot, cut into matchsticks
  1 small red pepper, cut into matchsticks
  2 cups finely shredded chinese cabbage
  1 cup bean sprouts
  ¼ cup coarsely chopped vietnamese mint leaves
  ¼ cup coarsely chopped fresh cilantro
  ¼ cup coarsely chopped raw unsalted peanuts
  2 tablespoons fried shallots

VIETNAMESE DRESSING
  ¼ cup lime juice
  2 tablespoons fish sauce
  1 tablespoon superfine sugar
  1 tablespoon water
  2 teaspoons sesame oil

1 Preheat oven to 425°F. Grease six-hole (¾ cup) texas muffin pan.
2 Spray wonton wrappers with oil; line each pan hole with three wrappers, oil-side up, overlapping slightly to form cups. Bake about 7 minutes or until browned lightly and crisp.
3 Meanwhile, make vietnamese dressing by placing ingredients in screw-top jar; shake well.
4 Combine chicken, carrot, pepper, chinese cabbage, sprouts, herbs, nuts and dressing in large bowl.
5 Divide chicken salad among wonton cups; sprinkle with fried shallots.

prep + cook time 27 minutes (+ cooling) **serves** 6
nutritional count per wonton cup 10g total fat (1.9g saturated fat); 199 cal; 7g carbohydrate; 19.2g protein; 2.2g fiber

chicken and mushroom party pies

1 tablespoon olive oil
1 small yellow onion chopped finely
1 clove garlic, crushed
14 ounces ground chicken
3½ ounces mushrooms, chopped finely
2 teaspoons plain (all-purpose) flour
¾ cup cream
2 tablespoons finely chopped fresh chives
3 sheets ready-rolled shortcrust pastry
1 egg, beaten lightly
2 sheets ready-rolled puff pastry
2 teaspoons sesame seeds

1 Heat oil in medium frying pan; cook onion and garlic, stirring, until onion softens. Add chicken and mushrooms; cook, stirring, until chicken changes color. Add flour; cook, stirring, 1 minute. Gradually stir in cream; cook, stirring, until mixture boils and thickens. Stir in chives; cool.
2 Preheat oven to 400°F. Grease two 12-hole (2 tablespoons) deep flat-based tart pans.
3 Cut twenty-four 2¾-inch rounds from shortcrust pastry; press into pan holes. Brush edges with a little of the egg. Spoon chicken mixture into pastry.
4 Cut twenty-four 2½-inch rounds from puff pastry; top pies with puff pastry lids. Press edges firmly to seal; brush lids with remaining egg, sprinkle with sesame seeds. Cut a small slit in top of each pie.
5 Bake about 20 minutes or until browned lightly. Stand pies in pan 5 minutes before serving.

prep + cook time 55 minutes **serves** 24
nutritional count per pie 14.5g total fat (7.4g saturated fat); 214 cal; 14.8g carbohydrate; 6g protein; 0.8g fiber

tip We used ground chicken breast for this recipe.

spanish chicken pie

5½ ounces cured chorizo sausage, sliced thinly
1½ pounds boneless chicken thighs,
    chopped coarsely
1 medium red onion, chopped coarsely
2 celery stalks, trimmed, chopped coarsely
8 ounces roasted red pepper, chopped coarsely
1 small fennel bulb, trimmed, sliced thinly
2 cloves garlic, crushed
½ teaspoon saffron threads
3 teaspoons mild paprika
¼ cup tomato paste
¾ cup water
½ cup seeded black olives
2 medium potatoes, unpeeled, sliced thinly

1 Heat large saucepan; cook chorizo, turning, until crisp. Remove from pan. Cook chicken, in batches, until browned all over. Remove from pan.
2 Add onion, celery, pepper, fennel and garlic to pan; cook, stirring, until softened. Add saffron, paprika, paste and the water; bring to a boil. Return chicken and chorizo to pan. Reduce heat, simmer, uncovered, about 15 minutes or until chicken is cooked through and sauce thickens. Stir in olives. Transfer to 6-cup ovenproof dish.
3 Meanwhile, preheat oven to 425°F. Arrange potato slices, slightly overlapping, over chicken mixture. Bake, uncovered, about 45 minutes or until potatoes are tender.

prep + cook time 1 hour 30 minutes **serves** 4
nutritional count per serving 23.5g total fat
(7.7g saturated fat); 490 cal; 28.9g carbohydrate;
38.1g protein; 5.8g fiber

chicken, bacon & blue cheese jalousie

1 tablespoon olive oil
3 bacon slices, chopped coarsely
1 small leek, sliced thinly
1 cup coarsely chopped barbecued chicken
4½ ounces blue cheese
2 sheets puff pastry
1 egg, beaten lightly

1 Preheat oven to 425°F. Line oven tray with parchment paper.
2 Heat half the oil in large frying pan; cook bacon until crisp. Drain on absorbent paper.
3 Heat remaining oil in same pan; cook leek, stirring, until tender. Combine leek in large bowl with bacon, chicken and cheese.

4 Cut each pastry sheet into two rectangles, one slightly larger than the other. Place smaller rectangles on tray. Top with chicken mixture, leaving a ½-inch border. Brush edges lightly with egg.
5 Gently fold larger pastry rectangles in half lengthwise. Cut through folded edge of pastry at ½-inch intervals, leaving a ½-inch border. Carefully unfold cut pastry strip, place over filling. Press edges of pastry together; brush lightly with egg.
6 Bake about 25 minutes or until browned.

prep + cook time 45 minutes **serves** 6
nutritional count per serving 29.3g total fat (7.9g saturated fat); 446 cal; 20.9g carbohydrate; 24.3g protein; 1.6g fiber

serving suggestion Serve with arugula salad.

smoky paprika chicken tart

tip: You can use one quantity basic shortcrust pastry (page 6) instead of the store-bought pastry sheets.

1 teaspoon saffron threads
1 tablespoon boiling water
2 tablespoons olive oil
1 medium yellow onion, cut into thin wedges
1 medium red pepper, chopped finely
2 cloves garlic, crushed
1 cured chorizo sausage (6 ounces), sliced thinly
2 teaspoons smoked paprika
12½ ounces boneless chicken thighs, chopped coarsely
13 ounces canned diced tomatoes
2 tablespoons lemon juice
½ cup water
2 sheets shortcrust pastry
2 slices sourdough bread, torn into pieces
¾ ounces butter, melted
¼ cup finely grated manchego or parmesan cheese

1 Combine saffron and the boiling water in small heatproof bowl. Stand 5 minutes.
2 Heat oil in large frying pan; cook onion, pepper, garlic and chorizo, stirring, until browned. Add paprika, cook, stirring, until fragrant. Add chicken, undrained tomatoes, juice, the water and saffron mixture. Simmer, uncovered, about 10 minutes or until thickened. Season to taste; cool.
3 Oil 9½-inch round loose-based flan pan. Cut one pastry sheet in half. Join pieces to two sides of remaining pastry sheet. Lift pastry into pan, ease into side, trim edge; prick base all over with fork. Place on cookie sheet. Refrigerate 30 minutes.
4 Meanwhile, preheat oven to 400°F. Bake pastry case 15 minutes. Cool.
5 Spoon filling into pastry case. Combine bread and butter in bowl. Spoon over pie; sprinkle with cheese. Bake, uncovered, about 20 minutes or until browned. Stand pie 5 minutes before serving.

prep + cook time 1 hour 20 minutes (+ cooling & refrigeration) **serves** 6
nutritional count per serving 41.3g total fat (17.6g saturated fat); 641 cal; 41.6g carbohydrate; 24.8g protein; 3.5g fiber

chicken bastilla

1	tablespoon olive oil
1½	pounds boneless chicken thighs, chopped
2	medium red onions, sliced thinly
2	cloves garlic, crushed
1	fresh long green chili, chopped finely
½	teaspoon saffron threads
2	teaspoons ground cilantro
1	teaspoon ground ginger
1½	cups chicken stock
½	cup slivered almonds, roasted
3	eggs, beaten lightly
½	cup each coarsely chopped fresh cilantro and fresh flat-leaf parsley
¼	cup coarsely chopped fresh mint
2½	ounces butter, melted
8	sheets filo pastry
1	teaspoon confectioners' sugar
½	teaspoon ground cinnamon

1 Heat half the oil in large frying pan; cook chicken, in batches, stirring occasionally, about 5 minutes or until browned. Remove from pan.
2 Heat remaining oil in pan; cook onion, stirring, until softened. Add garlic, chili, and spices; cook, stirring, until fragrant. Add stock and chicken; bring to a boil. Reduce heat, simmer, uncovered, about 20 minutes or until liquid has almost evaporated. Transfer to bowl; cool 5 minutes. Stir in nuts, egg and herbs; season to taste.
3 Preheat oven to 400°F. Brush deep 8-inch round cake pan with a little butter. Line an oven tray with parchment paper.
4 Layer four sheets of pastry, brushing each with butter. Line cake pan with pastry, allowing edges to overhang. Repeat with remaining butter and pastry. Position pastry crossways over pastry in pan. Spoon chicken mixture into pan. Fold overlapping pastry over filling to enclose. Brush with butter.
5 Bake about 30 minutes or until browned. Turn pie onto tray. Bake about 15 minutes or until browned. Dust with sifted sugar and cinnamon.

prep + cook time 1 hour 45 minutes **serves** 6
nutritional count per serving 30.6g total fat (11.8g saturated fat); 467 cal; 14.6g carbohydrate; 33.1g protein; 2.4g fiber

cajun chicken and corn pies

1 tablespoon olive oil
1 medium yellow onion, chopped finely
1 trimmed corn cob, kernels removed
2 cloves garlic, crushed
2 teaspoons cajun seasoning
12½ ounces boneless chicken thighs,
  chopped coarsely
2 tablespoons plain (all-purpose) flour
1 cup chicken stock
2 tablespoons finely chopped fresh cilantro
2 sheets shortcrust pastry
1 egg, beaten lightly
4 fresh small serrano chilies

1 Heat oil in large frying pan; cook onion, corn and garlic, stirring, until onion softens. Add seasoning; cook, stirring, until fragrant. Add chicken; cook, stirring, until chicken changes color. Add flour; cook, stirring, 1 minute. Gradually stir in stock; stir over heat until mixture boils and thickens; season, cool. Stir in cilantro.

2 Preheat oven to 400°F. Oil four holes of six-hole (¾-cup) texas muffin pan.
3 Cut four 5-inch rounds from pastry; press into pan holes. Divide chicken mixture among pastry cases.
4 Cut four 3½-inch rounds from pastry; top chicken filling with pastry rounds. Press edges firmly to seal; brush tops with egg. Insert a chili into each pie.
5 Bake pies about 25 minutes or until browned. Stand pies in pan 5 minutes before serving.

prep + cook time 55 minutes (+ cooling) makes 4
nutritional count per serving 59.7g total fat (27.6g saturated fat); 1034 cal; 88g carbohydrate; 34.7g protein; 6.1g fiber

tip One corn cob will give about 1 cup kernels. You can substitute frozen or drained canned kernels.

chicken and leek strudel

1 tablespoon olive oil
1 medium yellow onion, chopped finely
1 medium leek, white part only, sliced thinly
1 large carrot, finely chopped
2 cloves garlic, crushed
1 pound boneless chicken thighs, chopped finely
2 tablespoons plain (all-purpose) flour
1¼ cups light cream
8 sheets filo pastry
2½ ounces butter, melted
⅓ cup ground almonds

1 Heat oil in large frying pan; cook onion, leek, carrot and garlic, stirring, until carrot softens. Add chicken; cook, stirring, until browned. Add flour; cook, stirring, 1 minute. Gradually stir in cream; cook, stirring, until mixture boils and thickens. Season to taste. Cool.
2 Preheat oven to 400°F.

3 Line large oven tray with parchment paper. Brush one pastry sheet with melted butter; sprinkle with a little of the almonds. Layer with remaining pastry, butter and almonds, ending with a pastry sheet.
4 Spoon chicken mixture along one long side of pastry, leaving a 2-inch border on each side. Roll to enclose filling, fold in sides, roll up. Transfer roll to tray; brush with butter. Bake about 25 minutes or until browned. Stand strudel on tray 5 minutes before serving.

prep + cook time 1 hour (+ cooling & standing)
serves 8
nutritional count per serving 32.6g total fat (16.8g saturated fat); 416 cal; 14.3g carbohydrate; 16.1g protein; 2.6g fiber

tip It is fine to use just one 10½ fluid ounces carton of cream for this recipe.

thai green curry chicken pies

1 tablespoon vegetable oil
1 pound boneless chicken thighs, chopped coarsely
1 medium potato, chopped coarsely
1 tablespoon thai green curry paste
⅔ cup light coconut milk
⅔ cup water
1 tablespoon lime juice
3 ounces green beans, trimmed, chopped coarsely
2 tablespoons finely chopped fresh cilantro
2 sheets shortcrust pastry
1 egg, beaten lightly

1 Heat oil in large saucepan; cook chicken, stirring, until browned all over. Add potato and paste, cook, stirring, until fragrant. Add coconut milk, the water and juice; bring to a boil. Reduce heat, simmer, uncovered, about 10 minutes or until potato is tender and sauce is thick. Remove from heat, stir in beans and cilantro; season to taste. Cool 30 minutes.
2 Preheat oven to 400°F. Oil four holes of six-hole (¾-cup) texas muffin pan. Cut four 5-inch rounds and four 3½-inch rounds from pastry. Line base and side of holes with larger rounds. Divide chicken mixture among pastry cases.
3 Brush one side of smaller rounds with egg. Place egg side down over filling. Press edges to seal; brush tops with egg. Use pastry scraps to decorate pies. Bake pies about 45 minutes or until browned lightly.

prep + cook time 1 hour 25 minutes **makes** 4
nutritional count per serving 41.2g total fat (18.4g saturated fat); 677 cal; 43.7g carbohydrate; 32.2g protein; 3.1g fiber

chicken, mushroom and gnocchi pie

1 tablespoon olive oil
1 pound boneless chicken thighs,
    chopped coarsely
1 ounce butter
1 medium yellow onion, chopped finely
2 cloves garlic, sliced thinly
9½ ounces mixed mushrooms, sliced thinly
3 sprigs fresh thyme
1 tablespoon plain (all-purpose) flour
⅓ cup dry white wine
½ cup chicken stock
⅓ cup light cream
¼ cup coarsely chopped fresh flat-leaf parsley
1 pound gnocchi
½ cup finely grated parmesan cheese

1 Preheat oven to 425°F. Oil 6-cup ovenproof dish.
2 Heat oil in large frying pan; cook chicken until browned all over. Remove from pan.
3 Heat butter in same pan; cook onion, garlic, mushrooms and thyme until vegetables are tender. Add flour; cook, stirring, until mixture bubbles and thickens. Stir in wine, stock, cream and chicken. Bring to a boil, stirring until mixture boils and thickens slightly. Discard thyme. Stir in parsley; season to taste. Pour mixture into dish.
4 Meanwhile, cook gnocchi in large saucepan of boiling salted water about 3 minutes or until gnocchi float. Drain well.
5 Spoon gnocchi over filling. Sprinkle with cheese. Bake uncovered, about 20 minutes or until browned lightly.

prep + cook time 55 minutes **serves** 4
nutritional count per serving 32g total fat (15g saturated fat); 629 cal; 42.7g carbohydrate; 36.8g protein; 5.6g fiber

meat pies

chunky pork and fennel pie

- 2 pounds diced pork shoulder
- ⅓ cup plain (all-purpose) flour
- 2 tablespoons olive oil
- 1 large yellow onion, chopped coarsely
- 1 large carrot, chopped coarsely
- 1 stick celery, trimmed, chopped coarsely
- 1 large fennel bulb, sliced thinly
- 2 cloves garlic, crushed
- 2 teaspoons chopped fresh thyme
- 1⅓ cups chicken stock
- 2 tablespoons chopped fennel tops
- 1 tablespoon wholegrain mustard
- 1 egg, beaten lightly
- ¼ teaspoon fennel seeds

FENNEL PASTRY
- 3 cups plain (all-purpose) flour
- 1 teaspoon fennel seeds
- 6½ ounces butter, chopped
- 2 eggs
- ¼ cup iced water, approximately

1 Toss pork in flour; shake away excess. Heat oil in large saucepan; cook pork, in batches, until browned; remove from pan.

2 Add onion, carrot, celery and fennel to pan; cook, stirring, until softened. Add garlic and thyme; cook, stirring, until fragrant. Return pork to pan with stock; bring to a boil. Simmer, covered, 1½ hours. Simmer, uncovered, about 20 minutes or until mixture is slightly thickened. Stir in fennel tops and mustard; season to taste, cool.

3 Meanwhile, make fennel pastry.

4 Preheat oven to 350°F. Oil deep 9½-inch pie dish (6-cups).

5 Roll half the pastry between sheets of parchment paper until large enough to line dish. Press pastry into side; trim edge. Prick base with fork. Cover pastry with parchment paper, fill with dried beans or rice. Bake 15 minutes. Remove paper and beans, bake further 10 minutes or until browned. Cool.

6 Spoon pork mixture into pastry case. Brush edge of pastry with egg. Roll remaining pastry until large enough to cover top of dish, place over filling; pinch edges together, trim. Brush with egg; sprinkle with seeds. Cut several steam holes in pastry.

7 Place pie on cookie sheet; bake about 30 minutes or until browned.

FENNEL PASTRY Process flour, seeds and butter until crumbly. Add eggs and enough of the water to make ingredients just come together. Knead pastry on floured surface until smooth, enclose with plastic wrap; refrigerate 30 minutes.

prep + cook time 3 hours 30 minutes (+ refrigeration & cooling) **serves** 6
nutritional count per serving 43.8g total fat (22.3g saturated fat); 869 cal; 66.1g carbohydrate; 50.1g protein; 6.3g fiber

serving suggestion Serve with a green salad.

chunky beef and mushroom pies

1¼ pounds beef chuck steak, chopped coarsely
2 tablespoons plain (all-purpose) flour
2 tablespoons olive oil
1 small yellow onion, chopped finely
2 cloves garlic, crushed
4 ounces mushrooms, chopped coarsely
13 ounces canned crushed tomatoes
¾ cup beef stock
2 tablespoons tomato paste
2 tablespoons worcestershire sauce
3 sheets shortcrust pastry
2 sheets puff pastry
1 egg, beaten lightly

TOMATO SAUCE
1 tablespoon olive oil
1 medium yellow onion, chopped coarsely
2 tablespoons light brown sugar
1½ pounds canned crushed tomatoes
1 teaspoon ground allspice
2 tablespoons tomato paste
¼ cup white wine vinegar

1 Coat beef in flour; shake off excess. Heat half the oil in large saucepan; cook beef, in batches, until browned. Remove from pan.

2 Heat remaining oil in same pan; cook onion, garlic and mushrooms, stirring, until vegetables soften. Return beef to pan with undrained tomatoes, stock, paste and sauce; bring to a boil. Reduce heat; simmer, covered, 1 hour. Uncover; simmer about 15 minutes or until thickened slightly. Season to taste; cool.

3 Meanwhile, make tomato sauce.

4 Oil six ⅔-cup pie pans; place on cookie sheet. Cut six 5¼-inch rounds from shortcrust pastry. Ease pastry into pans, press into base and sides; trim edges. Refrigerate 30 minutes.

5 Preheat oven to 400°F.

6 Line pastry with parchment paper; fill with dried beans or rice. Bake 10 minutes; remove paper and beans. Bake further 5 minutes; cool.

7 Cut six 4½-inch rounds from puff pastry. Fill pastry cases with beef filling; brush edges with egg. Top with puff pastry rounds; press edges to seal. Brush tops with egg; cut steam holes in tops. Bake about 25 minutes or until browned lightly. Serve pies with tomato sauce.

TOMATO SAUCE Heat oil in medium saucepan; cook onion, stirring, until soft. Add sugar, undrained tomatoes and allspice; bring to a boil. Reduce heat; simmer, uncovered, stirring occasionally, about 30 minutes or until mixture thickens. Stir in paste and vinegar; cook, uncovered, 5 minutes. Blend or process sauce until smooth. Push through fine sieve into medium bowl; discard solids. Cool.

prep + cook time 2 hours (+ refrigeration) makes 6
nutritional count per pie (with sauce) 53.8g total fat
(17.1g saturated fat); 955 cal; 77.9g carbohydrate; 36.6g
protein; 7.5g fiber

beef and lentil pies with mashed sweet potato

1 tablespoon olive oil
1 medium yellow onion, chopped finely
2 cloves garlic, crushed
1 pound ground beef
1 tablespoon ground cumin
2 teaspoons ground cilantro
2 tablespoons tomato paste
1 cup beef stock
12½ ounces canned brown lentils, rinsed, drained
⅓ cup coarsely chopped fresh cilantro
1 medium sweet potato, chopped coarsely
1 medium potato, chopped coarsely
¾ ounce butter
2 tablespoons milk
½ teaspoon cumin seeds

1 Preheat oven to 425°F.
2 Heat oil in large saucepan; cook onion and garlic, stirring, until onion softens. Add beef; cook, stirring, until browned. Add spices; cook, stirring, until fragrant. Add paste, stock and lentils. Bring to a boil; simmer, uncovered, about 10 minutes or until thickened slightly. Stir in cilantro; season to taste.
3 Meanwhile, boil, steam or microwave the white and sweet potatoes until tender; drain. Mash vegetables in large bowl with butter and milk until smooth; season to taste.
4 Spoon mixture into four 1¼-cup ovenproof dishes. Top with mash. Sprinkle with seeds.
5 Bake pies about 20 minutes or until browned.

prep + cook time 55 minutes **makes** 4
nutritional count per serving 19g total fat (8.3g saturated fat); 414cal; 25.7g carbohydrate; 32.8g protein; 5.1g fiber

chili beef pies with cornbread topping

1 tablespoon olive oil
1 medium yellow onion, chopped finely
11 ounces ground beef
1½ teaspoons mexican chili powder
1 tablespoon plain (all-purpose) flour
12 ounces bottled chunky mild salsa
½ cup chicken stock
2 sheets shortcrust pastry
½ cup polenta
½ cup self-raising flour
½ cup coarsely grated cheddar cheese
⅔ cup buttermilk
1 egg, beaten lightly
¾ ounce butter, melted
¼ cup coarsely grated cheddar cheese

1   Heat oil in large frying pan; cook onion, stirring, until soft. Add beef; cook, stirring, until browned. Add chili powder; cook, stirring, until fragrant. Stir in flour, salsa and stock; bring to a boil, stirring; simmer, uncovered, 10 minutes. Season; cool.
2   Preheat oven to 400°F. Oil four 1-cup round pie pans. Cut four 6½-inch rounds from pastry. Lift pastry into pans, ease into bases and sides, trim edges; prick bases with fork. Refrigerate 20 minutes. Place pie pans on cookie sheet; bake 10 minutes. Cool.
3   Divide beef mixture among pastry cases. Combine polenta, flour and cheese in medium bowl. Stir in combined buttermilk, egg and butter. Spoon polenta mixture onto pies; sprinkle the tops with cheese.
4   Stand pans on cookie sheet, bake about 20 minutes or until browned lightly. Stand pies 5 minutes before serving.

prep + cook time 1 hour 20 minutes
(+ cooling & refrigeration) **makes** 4
nutritional count per serving 48.3g total fat
(23.9g saturated fat); 884 cal; 72.9g carbohydrate;
37.6g protein; 4.7g fiber

argentinean empanadas

2 tablespoons olive oil
1½ pounds beef chuck steak, chopped coarsely
1 medium yellow onion, chopped finely
2 teaspoons plain (all-purpose) flour
2 teaspoons ground cumin
1 teaspoon each ground cilantro and sweet paprika
2 cups beef stock
4 sheets shortcrust pastry
4 large green olives, seeded, sliced thinly
2 hard-boiled eggs, chopped coarsely
1 egg, beaten lightly
11 ounces bottled roasted pepper strips

1 Heat half the oil in large saucepan; cook beef, in batches, until browned. Remove from pan.
2 Heat remaining oil in same pan; cook onion, stirring, until softened. Add flour and spices; cook, stirring, 1 minute. Gradually stir in stock. Return beef to pan; bring to a boil. Simmer, covered, over low heat for 2 hours. Season to taste; cool.

3 Preheat oven to 425°F. Oil and line oven tray.
4 Cut eight 5½-inch rounds from pastry. Divide mixture among rounds. Top with olive and hard-boiled egg; seal pastry over filling. Pinch pastry edges together; place on oven tray. Brush with beaten egg. Bake about 25 minutes or until browned. Stand empanadas 5 minutes before serving.
5 Meanwhile, blend or process pepper strips until smooth. Serve with empanadas.

prep + cook time 3 hours makes 8
nutritional count per serving 36.7g total fat (15.7g saturated fat); 619 cal; 25.7g carbohydrate; 32.8g protein; 5.1g fiber

asian beef and eggplant cups

  1 tablespoon peanut oil
  4 cloves garlic, sliced thinly
1½-inch piece ginger, grated
  1 fresh long red chili, halved, sliced thinly
  1 medium eggplant, chopped finely
  1 pound ground beef
 ¼ cup plum sauce
  2 tablespoons dark soy sauce
  2 scallions, sliced thinly
18 sheets spring roll pastry
cooking-oil spray

1 Heat oil in large saucepan; cook garlic, ginger, chili and eggplant, stirring, until tender. Add beef, cook, stirring, until browned.
2 Add sauces and onion; bring to a boil, simmer, uncovered, 5 minutes. Cool.
3 Meanwhile, preheat oven to 400°F. Oil six-hole (¾-cup) texas muffin pan.
4 Cut each pastry sheet into 5½-inch squares. Layer 3 squares, spraying each with oil, overlapping to make a star pattern. Place in pan hole; spray with oil. Repeat with remaining pastry. Spoon filling into cases.
5 Bake about 20 minutes or until browned.

prep + cook time 50 minutes (+ cooling) **makes** 6
nutritional count per serving 10.7g total fat (3.4g saturated fat); 270 cal; 22.7g carbohydrate; 19.7g protein; 2.4g fiber

beef shiraz pies

1½ pounds beef chuck steak, chopped coarsely
2 tablespoons plain (all-purpose) flour
¼ cup olive oil
1 medium yellow onion, chopped finely
1 medium carrot, chopped finely
2 stalks celery, trimmed, chopped finely
2 cloves garlic, crushed
½ cup dry red wine
½ cup beef stock
13 ounces canned diced tomatoes
2 tablespoons fresh thyme leaves
1 egg, beaten lightly

SOUR CREAM PASTRY
2¼ cups plain (all-purpose) flour
4 ounces cold butter, chopped coarsely
½ cup sour cream

1 Preheat oven to 350°F. Oil six-hole (¾-cup) texas muffin pan.
2 Toss beef in flour, shake away excess. Heat half the oil in large frying pan; cook beef, in batches, until browned. Transfer beef to 12-cup ovenproof dish.
3 Heat remaining oil in same pan; cook onion, carrot, celery and garlic, stirring, until softened. Add wine; bring to a boil. Stir in stock, undrained tomatoes and thyme; bring to a boil. Pour over beef. Cook, covered, 2 hours. Season to taste; cool.
4 Meanwhile, make sour cream pastry.
5 Roll two-thirds of the pastry between sheets of parchment paper until large enough to cut six 5-inch rounds; press pastry into pan holes. Brush edges with egg. Divide beef mixture among pastry cases.
6 Cut six 3½-inch rounds from remaining pastry; place pastry over filling. Press edges firmly to seal; brush tops with egg. Cut a small slit in top of each pie.
7 Bake pies about 30 minutes or until browned. Stand pies 5 minutes before serving.

SOUR CREAM PASTRY Process flour and butter until crumbly. Add sour cream; process until ingredients barely cling together. Knead dough on floured surface until smooth. Enclose in plastic wrap; refrigerate 30 minutes.

prep + cook time 3 hours
(+ cooling & refrigeration) makes 6
nutritional count per serving 45.7g total fat
(21.6g saturated fat); 766 cal; 46.5g carbohydrate;
37.1g protein; 4.4g fiber

notes Sour cream pastry is lighter in texture but richer in flavor than basic shortcrust pastry. It is extremely easy to handle and may be used for both savory and sweet pies.
We used shiraz for this recipe, but you can use any red wine you like.

veal and tomato pies with gremolata

1½ pounds diced veal
2 tablespoons plain (all-purpose) flour
2 tablespoons olive oil
1 large yellow onion, sliced thinly
2 cloves garlic, crushed
½ cup dry white wine
¾ cup chicken stock
13 ounces canned diced tomatoes
2 tablespoons tomato paste
2 dried bay leaves
2 sheets shortcrust pastry
1 egg, beaten lightly
2 teaspoons finely grated lemon rind
¼ cup finely chopped fresh flat-leaf parsley
2 cloves garlic, crushed, extra

1   Coat veal in flour; shake off excess. Heat half the oil in large saucepan; cook veal, in batches, until browned. Remove from pan.
2   Heat remaining oil in same pan; cook onion and garlic, stirring, until onion softens. Add wine; boil, uncovered, stirring, until liquid evaporates. Return veal to pan with stock, undrained tomatoes, paste and bay leaves; bring to a boil. Reduce heat; simmer, covered, 1 hour. Uncover; simmer, about 45 minutes or until veal is tender and mixture is thick. Discard bay leaves. Season to taste; cool.
3   Preheat oven to 400°F.
4   Spoon veal mixture into four 1-cup ovenproof dishes. Cut four 5½-inch rounds from pastry. Lift pastry over dishes, pressing edges. Cut a slit in tops; brush with egg. Bake about 20 minutes. Serve with combined rind, parsley and extra garlic.

prep + cook time 2 hours
(+ refrigeration & cooling) **serves** 4
nutritional count per serving 25g total fat
(11.7g saturated fat); 515 cal; 32.4g carbohydrate;
38.4g protein; 3.3g fiber

tip You can use one quantity parmesan pastry (page 97) or one quantity basic shortcrust pastry (page 6) instead of the store-bought pastry sheets.

cottage pie

2 tablespoons olive oil
1 medium yellow onion, chopped finely
1 medium carrot, chopped finely
1 pound ground beef
2 tablespoons plain (all-purpose) flour
¾ cup beef stock
2 tablespoons ketchup
1 tablespoon worcestershire sauce
2 tablespoons finely chopped parsley
2 sheets shortcrust pastry
1¼ pounds potatoes, peeled, chopped coarsely
1½ ounces butter
½ cup hot milk
⅓ cup coarsely grated cheddar cheese

1 Heat oil in large frying pan; cook onion and carrot, stirring, until soft. Add beef, cook, stirring, until beef changes color. Add flour; cook, stirring, 1 minute. Gradually stir in combined stock and sauces; stir over heat until mixture boils and thickens. Simmer, uncovered, 10 minutes; stir in parsley, season to taste, cool.
2 Preheat oven to 400°F. Oil 9½-inch loose-based tart pan. Cut one sheet of pastry in half. Join pieces to two sides of remaining pastry sheet. Lift pastry into pan, ease into base and side, trim edge; prick base all over with fork. Place on an oven tray. Refrigerate 20 minutes.
3 Bake pastry case 15 minutes. Cool. Spoon beef mixture into pastry case.
4 Boil or steam potato about 20 minutes or until soft. Add butter and milk; mash until smooth, season to taste. Spoon mash over beef mixture; sprinkle with cheese.
5 Bake, uncovered, about 20 minutes or until browned. Stand pie 5 minutes before serving.

prep + cook time 1 hour 15 minutes
(+ cooling & refrigeration) **serves** 6
nutritional count per serving 35.8g total fat
(16.9g saturated fat); 606 cal; 43.8g carbohydrate;
26.2g protein; 3.4g fiber

tip You can use one quantity basic shortcrust pastry (page 6) instead of the store-bought pastry sheets.

beef pies with polenta tops

1 pound 2 ounces beef chuck steak, cut into 1½-in pieces
1 tablespoon plain (all-purpose) flour
2 tablespoons olive oil
1 small yellow onion, chopped finely
2 cloves garlic, crushed
3½ ounces button mushrooms, halved
½ cup dry red wine
½ cup beef stock
1 cup canned crushed tomatoes
1 small red pepper, chopped coarsely
¼ cup seeded black olives
¼ cup coarsely chopped, drained sun-dried tomatoes in oil
⅓ cup coarsely chopped fresh basil
2 sheets ready-rolled shortcrust pastry
1 large potato, chopped coarsely
¾ ounce butter
1 tablespoon milk
¼ cup finely grated parmesan cheese

SOFT POLENTA
¼ cup chicken stock
¾ cup milk
¼ cup polenta
¼ cup finely grated parmesan cheese

1 Coat beef in flour; shake off excess. Heat half the oil in large saucepan; cook beef, in batches, until browned.
2 Heat remaining oil in same pan; cook onion, garlic and mushrooms, stirring, until vegetables soften. Add wine; bring to a boil. Return beef to pan with stock and crushed tomatoes; bring to a boil. Reduce heat; simmer, covered, 1 hour. Uncover, stir in pepper, olives and sun-dried tomato; simmer 15 minutes or until sauce thickens; cool. Stir in basil.
3 Preheat oven to 350°F. Grease six-hole (¾-cup) texas muffin pan.
4 Make soft polenta.
5 Meanwhile, boil, steam or microwave potato until tender; drain. Mash potato with butter and milk in medium bowl until smooth.
6 Gently swirl hot polenta mixture into hot potato mixture.
7 Cut six 4½ inch rounds from shortcrust pastry; press into pan holes. Divide beef mixture among pastry cases; top with potato and polenta mixture, sprinkle with cheese.
8 Bake, in oven, about 30 minutes. Stand pies in pan 5 minutes before using a palette knife to loosen pie from side of pan and ease out.

SOFT POLENTA Combine stock and milk in small saucepan; bring to a boil. Gradually stir polenta into stock mixture. Reduce heat; cook, stirring, about 5 minutes or until polenta thickens. Stir in cheese.

prep + cook time 2 hours 35 minutes serves 6
nutritional count per serving 32.3g total fat (14.6g saturated fat); 606 cal; 44.8g carbohydrate; 28.6g protein; 4.5g fiber

beef and onion party pies

1 tablespoon vegetable oil
1 medium yellow onion, chopped finely
1 pound ground beef
2 tablespoons tomato paste
2 tablespoons worcestershire sauce
2 tablespoons powdered gravy mix
¾ cup water
3 sheets ready-rolled shortcrust pastry
1 egg, beaten lightly
2 sheets ready-rolled puff pastry

1 Heat oil in large frying pan; cook onion, stirring, until onion softens. Add beef; cook, stirring, until beef changes color. Add paste, sauce, and blended gravy powder and the water; bring to a boil, stirring. Reduce heat; simmer, uncovered, about 10 minutes or until thickened slightly; cool.

2 Preheat oven to 400°F. Grease two 12-hole (2 tablespoons) deep flat-based tart pans.

3 Cut twenty-four 2¾ inch rounds from shortcrust pastry; press into pan holes. Divide beef mixture among pastry cases. Brush edges with a little of the egg.

4 Cut twenty-four 2½ inch rounds from puff pastry; top pies with puff pastry lids. Press edges firmly to seal; brush lids with remaining egg. Cut a small slit in top of each pie.

5 Bake about 20 minutes or until browned lightly. Stand pies in pan 5 minutes before serving.

prep + cook time 1 hour **serves** 24
nutritional count per serving 11.2g total fat (5.4g saturated fat); 189 cal; 15.5g carbohydrate; 6.4g protein; 0.7g fiber

moussaka timbales

¼ cup olive oil
1 medium yellow onion, chopped finely
2 cloves garlic, crushed
1 pound 2 ounces ground lamb
14 ounce can diced tomatoes
1 tablespoon tomato paste
½ cup dry white wine
1 teaspoon ground cinnamon
¼ teaspoon ground nutmeg
¼ cup coarsely chopped fresh flat-leaf parsley
¼ cup roasted pine nuts
2 small eggplants

1 Heat 1 tablespoon of the oil in large frying pan; cook onion and garlic, stirring, until onion softens. Add lamb; cook, stirring, until lamb changes color. Stir in undrained tomatoes, paste, wine and spices; bring to a boil. Reduce heat; simmer, uncovered, about 20 minutes or until liquid has evaporated. Cool; stir in parsley and nuts.
2 Meanwhile, slice eggplant lengthwise into ⅛ inch thin slices using sharp knife, mandolin or V-slicer. Mix eggplant slices with remaining oil; cook on heated grill plate until browned lightly. Cool.
3 Preheat oven to 350°F. Grease six-hole (¾-cup) texas muffin pan. Line each pan hole with eggplant slices, overlapping slightly and extending 1½ inch above edge of hole. Divide lamb mixture among eggplant cases. Fold eggplant over to enclose filling.
4 Bake about 10 minutes. Stand in pan 5 minutes before serving, top-side down. Sprinkle with chopped fresh flat-leaf parsley.

prep + cook time 1 hour 15 minutes serves 6
nutritional count per serving 19.9g total fat (4g saturated fat); 302 cal; 6.3g carbohydrate; 19.8g protein; 3.7g fiber

serving suggestion Accompany with tzatziki, a Greek dip made from yogurt, diced cucumber and garlic.

yorkshire puddings with beef and red wine stew

1 pound 12 ounces beef chuck steak, cut into 1½-inch pieces
2 tablespoons plain (all-purpose) flour
⅓ cup olive oil
1½ ounces butter
6 shallots, halved
2 cloves garlic, crushed
5½ ounces button mushrooms, halved
1 large carrot, chopped coarsely
1 cup dry red wine
2 tablespoons tomato paste
1 cup beef stock
2 tablespoons worcestershire sauce
2 sprigs fresh thyme
¼ cup coarsely chopped fresh chives

YORKSHIRE PUDDING BATTER
⅓ cup plain (all-purpose) flour
¼ teaspoon salt
⅓ cup milk
1 egg

1 Coat beef in flour; shake off excess. Heat 2 tablespoons of the oil in large saucepan; cook beef, in batches, until browned all over.
2 Melt half the butter in same pan; cook shallot, garlic, mushrooms and carrot, stirring, until vegetables soften. Add wine; bring to a boil. Return beef to pan with paste, stock, sauce and thyme; bring to a boil. Reduce heat; simmer, covered, 1¼ hours. Uncover; simmer about 15 minutes or until sauce thickens. Stir in chives.
3 Meanwhile, make yorkshire pudding batter.
4 Preheat oven to 475°F. Melt remaining butter; divide combined melted butter and remaining oil among four holes of six-hole (¾-cup) texas muffin pan. Heat pan in oven 3 minutes. Remove pan from oven; immediately divide batter among hot pan holes.
5 Return pan to oven; bake about 12 minutes or until puddings are well browned. Serve puddings, top-side up, with stew; sprinkle with chopped fresh chives.

YORKSHIRE PUDDING BATTER Sift flour and salt into small bowl. Whisk in combined milk and egg until smooth. Pour into jug, cover; stand 20 minutes.

prep + cook time 2 hours 15 minutes serves 4
nutritional count per serving 38.2g total fat (12.8g saturated fat); 667 cal; 21.1g carbohydrate; 48.4g protein; 4.1g fiber

meat pie scrolls

1	tablespoon olive oil
1	small yellow onion, chopped finely
1	clove garlic, crushed
3	rindless bacon strips, chopped finely
10½	ounces ground beef
14	ounce can diced tomatoes
1	tablespoon tomato paste
2	tablespoons worcestershire sauce
½	cup beef stock
¼	cup coarsely chopped fresh flat-leaf parsley
2	cups self-raising flour
1	tablespoon superfine sugar
2	ounces butter, chopped coarsely
¾	cup milk
1	cup mozzarella cheese

1 Heat oil in large frying pan; cook onion, garlic and bacon, stirring, until onion softens. Add beef; cook, stirring, until beef changes color. Add undrained tomatoes, paste, sauce and stock; bring to a boil. Reduce heat; simmer, uncovered, about 20 minutes or until sauce thickens. Remove from heat; stir in parsley. Cool.
2 Preheat oven to 350°F. Grease two six-hole (¾-cup) texas muffin pans.
3 Sift flour and sugar into medium bowl; rub in butter with fingers. Stir in milk; mix to a soft, sticky dough. Knead dough on floured surface; roll dough out to 12 inch x 6 inch rectangle.
4 Spread beef mixture over dough; sprinkle with cheese. Roll dough tightly from one long side; trim ends. Cut roll into 12 slices; place one slice in each pan hole. Bake about 25 minutes. Serve top-side up.

prep + cook time 1 hour 15 minutes **serves** 12
nutritional count per serving 11.8g total fat (5.7g saturated fat); 257 cal; 22.4g carbohydrate; 14.5g protein; 1.6g fiber

lamb masala pies with raita

2 tablespoons vegetable oil
1 medium yellow onion, chopped finely
1½ pounds diced lamb
⅓ cup tikka masala paste
14 ounce can diced tomatoes
¼ cup water
½ cup cream
¼ cup coarsely chopped fresh cilantro
2 sheets ready-rolled shortcrust pastry
1 egg, beaten lightly
2 sheets ready-rolled puff pastry

RAITA
¾ cup yogurt
1 cucumber, seeded, chopped finely
2 tablespoons finely chopped fresh mint

1 Heat oil in large saucepan; cook onion, stirring, until onion softens. Add lamb; cook, stirring, until browned. Add paste; cook, stirring, until fragrant. Add undrained tomatoes, the water and cream; bring to a boil. Reduce heat; simmer, uncovered, about 25 minutes or until sauce thickens; cool. Stir in cilantro.
2 Preheat oven to 400°F. Grease six-hole (¾-cup) texas muffin pan.
3 Cut six 4½-inch rounds from shortcrust pastry; press into pan holes. Brush edges with a little of the egg. Divide lamb curry among pastry cases.
4 Cut six 3-inch rounds from puff pastry; top curry with puff pastry rounds. Press edges firmly to seal; brush tops with remaining egg. Cut a small slit in top of each pie.
5 Bake about 25 minutes. Stand pies in pan 5 minutes before serving.
6 Meanwhile, make raita by combining ingredients in small bowl.
7 Sprinkle lamb masala pies with fresh cilantro leaves; serve with raita.

prep + cook time 1 hour 25 minutes **serves** 6
nutritional count per serving 54g total fat (24.7g saturated fat); 830 cal; 52g carbohydrate; 32.2g protein; 5.1g fiber

mexican beef and bean pie

¼ cup olive oil
1½ pounds beef chuck steak, chopped coarsely
¼ cup plain (all-purpose) flour
1 medium yellow onion, chopped finely
1 ounce taco seasoning mix
2 cups bottled tomato pasta sauce
½ cup chicken stock
12½ ounces canned red kidney beans, rinsed, drained
1 cup corn chips

POLENTA PASTRY
1¼ cups plain (all-purpose) flour
⅓ cup polenta
2½ ounces butter, chopped coarsely
1 egg
2 tablespoons iced water, approximately

1 Preheat oven to 350°F. Oil 9½-inch round loose-based tart pan.
2 Heat half the oil in large saucepan; toss beef in flour, shake away excess. Cook beef, in batches, until browned. Transfer to 12-cup ovenproof dish. Heat remaining oil in same pan; cook onion, stirring, until softened. Add seasoning mix, cook, stirring, 1 minute. Gradually stir in sauce and stock; bring to a boil. Pour over beef. Bake, covered, 2 hours.
3 Stir beans into beef mixture; cook, uncovered, 10 minutes. Season to taste; cool.
4 Meanwhile, make pastry.
5 Roll pastry between sheets of parchment paper until large enough to line pan. Lift pastry into pan, press into side; trim edge. Place on cookie sheet, bake about 20 minutes or until browned lightly; cool.
6 Spoon filling into pastry case. Bake about 20 minutes or until heated through. Stand pie 5 minutes; serve topped with corn chips.

POLENTA PASTRY Process flour, polenta and butter until mixture is crumbly. Add egg and most of the water; process until ingredients just come together. Knead pastry on floured surface until smooth, enclose with plastic wrap; refrigerate pastry 30 minutes.

prep + cook time 2 hours 50 minutes
(+ cooling & refrigeration) serves 6
nutritional count per serving 34.1g total fat
(12.6g saturated fat); 650 cal; 50.1g carbohydrate;
39g protein; 7.3g fiber

serving suggestion Serve with guacamole and sour cream.

tomato, feta and pancetta frittata

6 slices pancetta, chopped coarsely
3½ ounces feta cheese, crumbled
¼ cup finely grated parmesan cheese
⅓ cup coarsely chopped fresh basil
6 eggs
⅔ cup cream
9 mini roma tomatoes, halved lengthwise

1 Preheat oven to 350°F. Grease six-hole (¾-cup) texas muffin pan; line bases with parchment paper.
2 Layer pancetta, cheeses and basil in pan holes. Whisk eggs and cream in medium bowl; pour into pan holes. Top each frittata with three tomato halves.
3 Bake about 25 minutes. Stand in pan 5 minutes before turning out.

prep + cook time 35 minutes **serves** 6
nutritional count per serving 24.1g total fat (13.3g saturated fat); 280 cal; 1.6g carbohydrate; 14.9g protein; 0.4g fiber

nachos

1 tablespoon olive oil
1 small yellow onion, chopped finely
1 clove garlic, crushed
14 ounces ground beef
1 fresh long red chili, chopped finely
1¼ ounces packet taco seasoning mix
14 ounce can diced tomatoes
1 tablespoon tomato paste
⅓ cup beef stock
16 ounce can mexican chili beans, rinsed, drained
¼ cup coarsely chopped fresh cilantro
8 ounces corn chips, chopped coarsely
1½ cups coarsely grated cheddar cheese

GUACAMOLE
1 large avocado, chopped coarsely
1 medium tomato, chopped finely
½ small red onion, chopped finely
1 tablespoon lime juice
1 tablespoon finely chopped fresh cilantro

1 Heat oil in large frying pan; cook onion and garlic, stirring, until onion softens. Add beef; cook, stirring, until beef changes color. Add chili and seasoning mix; cook, stirring, until fragrant.

2 Add undrained tomatoes, paste and stock; bring to a boil. Reduce heat; simmer, uncovered, 15 minutes. Add beans; cook, stirring, about 5 minutes or until thickened. Stir in cilantro. Cool.

3 Preheat oven to 400°F. Grease eight holes of two 6-hole (¾-cup) texas muffin pans; line greased pan holes with two criss-crossed 2 inch x 20 inch strips of parchment paper.

4 Combine corn chips and 1 cup of the cheese in small bowl; divide half the corn chip mixture among pan holes, pressing down firmly. Divide beef mixture among pan holes; top with remaining corn chip mixture, pressing down firmly. Sprinkle with remaining cheese. Bake about 15 minutes or until browned lightly.

5 Meanwhile, make guacamole by mashing avocado in medium bowl; stir in remaining ingredients.

6 Stand nachos in pan 5 minutes. Using parchment paper strips as lifters, carefully remove nachos from pan holes. Serve topped with guacamole; sprinkle with fresh cilantro leaves.

prep + cook time 1 hour 5 minutes **serves** 8
nutritional count per serving 27.7g total fat (11g saturated fat); 440 cal; 23.1g carbohydrate; 21.9g protein; 6.9g fiber

serving suggestion Accompany with lime wedges and sour cream.

spanish tortilla

1 pound 2 ounces potatoes, sliced thinly
1 tablespoon olive oil
1 medium yellow onion, sliced thinly
1 chorizo sausage (6 ounces), sliced thinly
4 scallions, chopped coarsely
5 eggs
1 cup cream
1 clove garlic, crushed
¾ cup coarsely grated cheddar cheese

1 Preheat oven to 350°F. Grease six-hole (¾-cup) texas muffin pan; line bases with parchment paper.
2 Boil, steam or microwave potato until tender; drain.
3 Meanwhile, heat oil in medium frying pan; cook yellow onion, stirring, until onion softens. Add chorizo; cook, stirring, until chorizo crisps. Stir in scallion; drain mixture on absorbent paper.
4 Whisk eggs in medium bowl with cream and garlic. Divide potato, chorizo mixture and cheese among pan holes. Pour egg mixture into pan holes.
5 Bake, in oven, about 30 minutes or until set. Stand tortillas in pan 5 minutes before turning out, top-side up.

prep + cook time 55 minutes **serves** 6
nutritional count per serving 39.1g total fat (20g saturated fat); 483 cal; 14.7g carbohydrate; 18.1g protein; 2.3g fiber

serving suggestion Serve tortillas with a spinach salad.

pizza muffins

4 bacon strips, chopped finely
4 scallions, chopped finely
3 slices bottled roasted red peppers, chopped finely
¾ cup mozzarella cheese
½ teaspoon dried chili flakes

BASIC MUFFIN MIX
2 cups self-raising flour
2¾ ounces butter, melted
1 egg
1 cup buttermilk

1 Preheat oven to 400°F. Grease 12-hole (⅓-cup) muffin pan.
2 Cook bacon in heated medium frying pan, stirring, until browned lightly. Add onion; cook, stirring, until onion softens. Cool.
3 Meanwhile make basic muffin mix.
4 Add peppers, cheese, chili and bacon mixture to basic muffin mix; mix gently to combine. Do not over-mix; mixture should be lumpy.
5 Divide mixture among holes. Bake, in oven, about 20 minutes. Stand muffins 5 minutes before turning, top-side up, onto wire rack. Serve muffins warm

BASIC MUFFIN MIX Sift flour into medium bowl; stir in combined butter, egg and buttermilk.

prep + cook time 45 minutes serves 12
nutritional count per serving 11.8g total fat (6.1g saturated fat); 222 cal; 17g carbohydrate; 10.7g protein; 2.9g fiber

serving suggestion Accompany warm muffins with butter.

prosciutto and feta baked eggs

12 slices prosciutto
¼ cup finely chopped drained sun-dried
  tomatoes in oil
1¾ ounces feta cheese, crumbled
2 tablespoons coarsely chopped fresh basil
2 tablespoons coarsely chopped fresh chives
6 eggs

1 Preheat oven to 400°F. Grease six-hole (⅓-cup) muffin pan.
2 Wrap one prosciutto slice around edge of each pan hole, lay another slice to cover bases; press firmly to seal edges to form a cup. Divide half the combined tomato, cheese and herbs among prosciutto cups. Break an egg into each cup. Sprinkle with remaining cheese mixture.
3 Bake about 12 minutes or until eggs are cooked. Remove carefully from pan. Serve top-side up.

prep + cook time 17 minutes **serves** 6
nutritional count per serving 9.4g total fat (3.6g saturated fat); 152 cal; 2.3g carbohydrate; 14.3g protein; 0.9g fiber

serving suggestion Accompany with cherry tomatoes.

prosciutto and roasted red pepper quiche

 6 slices prosciutto
 3 sheets ready-rolled shortcrust pastry
 4 slices bottled roasted red bell peppers,
    chopped coarsely
 ⅓ cup coarsely chopped fresh basil
 ¾ cup mozzarella cheese
 1 quantity quiche filling *(see crab, fennel and
    herb quiche recipe, page 108)*

1 Preheat oven to 400°F. Grease 12-hole (⅓-cup)
muffin pan.
2 Cook prosciutto in heated oiled large frying pan
until crisp. Cool; chop coarsely.
3 Cut twelve 3½-inch rounds from pastry; press
into pan holes. Divide combined prosciutto,
peppers, basil and cheese among pastry cases;
pour quiche filling into pastry cases.
4 Bake about 25 minutes. Stand in pan 5 minutes
before serving.

prep + cook time 50 minutes **serves** 12
nutritional count per serving 26.5g total fat
(14.8g saturated fat); 350 cal; 19.7g carbohydrate;
8.3g protein; 0.8g fiber

pork sausage and apple pie

1 tablespoon olive oil
1 medium yellow onion, chopped finely
1 baby fennel bulb, sliced thinly
6 thick pork and herb sausages
2 teaspoons plain (all-purpose) flour
1 cup chicken stock
2 teaspoons mild english mustard
1 medium apple, grated coarsely
2 tablespoons coarsely chopped fresh
   flat-leaf parsley
1 egg, beaten lightly

SHORTCRUST PASTRY
1½ cups plain (all-purpose) flour
2½ ounces cold butter, chopped coarsely
1 egg yolk
2 tablespoons iced water, approximately

1 Make shortcrust pastry.
2 Preheat oven to 400°F. Oil 6-cup ovenproof dish.
3 Heat oil in large frying pan; stir onion, fennel and meat squeezed from sausages until browned. Add flour; cook, stirring, until mixture bubbles and thickens. Gradually stir in stock and mustard, stir over heat until mixture boils and thickens, simmer, 5 minutes. Stir in apple and parsley; season. Spoon mixture into dish.
4 Roll pastry between sheets of parchment paper until large enough to cover dish. Top dish with pastry, brush with egg. Bake about 30 minutes or until pastry is browned.

SHORTCRUST PASTRY Process flour and butter until crumbly. Add egg yolk and most of the water; process until ingredients just come together. Knead pastry on floured surface until smooth, enclose with plastic wrap; refrigerate 30 minutes.

prep + cook time 1 hour (+ refrigeration) **serves** 4
nutritional count per serving 64.7g total fat (28.7g saturated fat); 931 cal; 53.8g carbohydrate; 32g protein; 6.2g fiber

beef and caramelized onion pies

   2 medium red onions
   2 tablespoons olive oil
   2 tablespoons brown sugar
   1 cup beer
   2 cloves garlic, crushed
6½ ounces button mushrooms, sliced thinly
   3 sprigs fresh thyme
   1 pound ground beef
¼ cup tomato paste
   2 teaspoons fresh thyme leaves
   1 sheet puff pastry, quartered
   1 egg, beaten lightly
   1 teaspoon brown sugar, extra

1 Preheat oven to 425°F.
2 Slice onions thinly, reserving four intact small slices. Heat half the oil in large frying pan; cook onion, stirring, until soft. Add sugar and ¼ cup of the beer; cook, stirring occasionally, about 10 minutes until onion caramelizes.
3 Meanwhile, heat remaining oil in large saucepan; cook garlic, mushrooms and thyme sprigs until soft. Add beef, cook, stirring, until browned. Add paste and remaining beer. Simmer, uncovered, about 10 minutes or until thickened slightly. Stir in caramelized onion and thyme leaves; season. Discard thyme sprigs.
4 Spoon mixture into four 1-cup ovenproof dishes. Top each with pastry; brush with egg. Sprinkle reserved onion slices with extra sugar, press gently into center of pastry. Place dishes on cookie sheet. Bake about 20 minutes or until pastry is puffed and browned.

prep + cook time 1 hour **makes** 4
nutritional count per serving 28.8g total fat
(6g saturated fat); 537 cal; 30.3g carbohydrate;
33.3g protein; 3.9g fiber

individual beef wellingtons

2 teaspoons olive oil
1½-pound piece beef tenderloin
6½ ounces button mushrooms
2 shallots, chopped coarsely
1 clove garlic, crushed
¾ ounce butter
1 tablespoon finely chopped fresh tarragon
1 tablespoon finely chopped fresh flat-leaf parsley
⅓ cup pâté
12 thin slices prosciutto
4 sheets puff pastry
1 egg, beaten lightly

1 Heat oil in large frying pan; season beef, cook over high heat until well browned all over. Remove from pan. Wrap tightly in plastic wrap to hold shape. Place on a plate; refrigerate 1 hour.

2 Meanwhile, process mushrooms, shallots and garlic until chopped finely. Heat butter in same pan; add mushroom mixture. Cook, stirring, until liquid has evaporated. Transfer to small bowl; season to taste, cool. Stir in tarragon and parsley.

3 Preheat oven to 425°F. Line cookie sheet with parchment paper; place wire rack over tray.

4 Cut beef into four, spread top of each with pâté. Put one slice prosciutto onto counter; overlap slightly with another slice and top with another slice in the center. Spread a quarter of the mushroom mixture evenly over center of prosciutto. Place beef, pâté-side up, on one short end of prosciutto. Enclose with prosciutto. Repeat with remaining prosciutto, mushroom mixture and beef.

5 Place beef in center of each pastry sheet, fold two sides over to enclose beef, press pastry onto sides of beef. Trim excess pastry away. Press edges of pastry together with a fork. Cut a small steam hole on top of each wellington. Decorate with pastry scraps.

6 Place wellingtons on wire rack; brush with egg. Bake about 20 minutes for medium beef. Stand wellingtons on rack for 10 minutes before serving.

prep + cook time 1 hour 20 minutes
(+ refrigeration) makes 4
nutritional count per serving 58.8g total fat
(10.8g saturated fat); 1046 cal; 61.5g carbohydrate; 66g
protein; 4g fiber

caramelized onion, fig and prosciutto tarts

1½ ounces butter
2 large yellow onions, sliced thinly
1 tablespoon brown sugar
2 sheets puff pastry
3 fresh figs, quartered
2½ ounces firm blue cheese, crumbled
4 thin slices prosciutto, halved
1 tablespoon balsamic glaze
¾ ounce baby arugula leaves

1 Preheat oven to 425°F. Oil and line cookie sheet.
2 Heat butter in medium pan; add onion, cook covered, over low heat, about 15 minutes, stirring occasionally, until onion is soft. Stir in sugar.

3 Meanwhile, quarter pastry sheets, place on cookie sheet. Fold in ½-inch borders; prick centers, bake pastry about 15 minutes or until browned.
4 Spread onion mixture into pastry cases, top with figs and cheese; bake about 3 minutes or until cheese is softened.
5 Top tarts with prosciutto, drizzle with balsamic glaze; sprinkle with arugula.

prep + cook time 35 minutes **serves** 8 as an entrée
nutritional count per serving 17.4g total fat (5.6g saturated fat); 271 cal; 21.2g carbohydrate; 6.8g protein; 1.8g fiber

tip Feta or goat's cheese can be used in place of the blue cheese.

spiced chorizo and bean pies

2 teaspoons olive oil
3 cured chorizo sausages, halved, sliced thinly
1 medium red onion, chopped finely
2 cloves garlic, crushed
¼ teaspoon dried chili flakes
1 teaspoon each smoked paprika and ground cumin
13 ounces canned crushed tomatoes
⅓ cup water
12½ ounces canned white beans, rinsed, drained
4 sheets filo pastry
1 ounce butter, melted

1 Preheat oven to 425°F. Oil four 1¼-cup ovenproof dishes.
2 Heat oil in large saucepan; cook chorizo until crisp. Remove from pan, reserving oil. Cook onion and garlic in same pan, stirring, until softened. Add spices; cook, stirring, until fragrant. Add undrained tomatoes, the water and beans. Simmer, uncovered, 5 minutes; season.
3 Spoon mixture into dishes.
4 Brush pastry sheets with butter. Scrunch and place over filling.
5 Bake pies about 15 minutes or until pastry is browned and crisp.

prep + cook time 45 minutes **makes** 4
nutritional count per serving 35.2g total fat (14.1g saturated fat); 447 cal; 16.1g carbohydrate; 15.6g protein; 4.1g fiber

chorizo and potato galette with green olives

2 sheets puff pastry
2 tablespoons olive oil
2 cloves garlic, chopped finely
½ teaspoon sweet paprika
2 teaspoons coarsely chopped fresh rosemary
2 small unpeeled potatoes
4 ounces cured chorizo sausage, sliced thinly
¼ small red onion, sliced thinly
⅓ cup roasted pepper strips
¾ cup drained marinated green olives
¼ cup fresh flat-leaf parsley leaves

1 Preheat oven to 425°F. Line two cookie sheets with parchment paper.
2 Place pastry on trays. Combine oil, garlic, paprika and rosemary in small bowl. Brush half the oil mixture over pastry, leaving a ½-inch border.
3 Slice potatoes thinly using mandolin or V-slicer. Top pastry pieces with single layer of potato; brush with remaining oil mixture; season.
4 Bake 10 minutes. Top with chorizo, onion and peppers; bake about 10 minutes or until pastry is crisp.
5 Top galettes with olives and parsley.

prep + cook time 30 minutes **serves** 4
nutritional count per serving 36.8g total fat (5.8g saturated fat); 540 cal; 41.5g carbohydrate; 9.9g protein; 3g fiber

lamb and rosemary pies with scone topping

2 teaspoons olive oil
5 thick lamb and rosemary sausages
1 medium yellow onion, chopped finely
1 tablespoon plain (all-purpose) flour
1¼ cups chicken stock
1 tablespoon honey
2 tablespoons coarsely chopped
   fresh rosemary
1 tablespoon milk
4 sprigs fresh rosemary

SCONE TOPPING
1 cup self-raising flour
2 ounces butter, chopped coarsely
¼ cup finely grated parmesan cheese
½ cup milk, approximately

1   Preheat oven to 400°F. Oil four 1¼-cup
ovenproof dishes.
2   Heat oil in large frying pan. Cook sausages until
browned and cooked through; slice thinly. Cook
onion in same pan, stirring, until tender. Add flour;
cook, stirring, until mixture bubbles and thickens.
Stir in stock, honey and chopped rosemary, stir
over heat until mixture boils and thickens; simmer
3 minutes. Return sausage to pan. Season.
3   Meanwhile, make scone topping.
4   Spoon hot filling into dishes. Top with scone
topping. Brush with milk; press a rosemary sprig
into top of each pie. Bake about 25 minutes or
until browned.

SCONE TOPPING Place flour in medium bowl;
rub in butter, stir in parmesan. Stir in enough milk
to make a soft sticky dough. Divide dough into
four, knead into rounds to fit dishes.

prep + cook time 55 minutes **makes** 4
nutritional count per serving 36.8g total fat
(19.2g saturated fat); 675 cal; 38.7g carbohydrate;
46.9g protein; 2g fiber

rogan josh lamb pie with cilantro chutney

tip Ask the butcher for lamb shoulder, as what is sold as diced lamb is sometimes from the leg and will not be as tender.

2 pounds diced lamb shoulder
⅓ cup plain (all-purpose) flour
2 tablespoons vegetable oil
2 medium yellow onions, sliced thinly
½ cup rogan josh curry paste
13 ounces canned diced tomatoes
2 cups salt-reduced beef stock
1 sheet puff pastry
2 teaspoons milk
¼ teaspoon cumin seeds

CILANTRO CHUTNEY
1 tablespoon lemon juice
1 teaspoon sugar
pinch ground cumin
1 fresh long green chili, chopped coarsely
1 cup firmly packed fresh cilantro leaves
1 cup firmly packed fresh mint leaves
½ cup thick yogurt

1 Toss lamb in flour, shake away excess. Heat oil in large saucepan; cook lamb, in batches, until well browned. Remove from pan. Add onion to same pan; cook, stirring, until softened.
2 Add paste to pan; cook, stirring, until fragrant. Return lamb to pan with undrained tomatoes and stock; bring to a boil, simmer, covered, 1½ hours. Simmer, uncovered, about 30 minutes or until tender. Season to taste; cool.
3 Preheat oven to 425°F.
4 Spoon curry into 9½-inch pie dish (6-cup). Score pastry in criss-cross pattern. Place pastry over filling; trim edge. Brush pastry with milk, sprinkle with seeds. Place on cookie sheet; bake, uncovered, about 30 minutes or until browned.
5 Meanwhile, make cilantro chutney.
6 Serve pie with chutney.

CILANTRO CHUTNEY Blend all ingredients until smooth; season to taste.

prep + cook time 3 hours (+ cooling) **serves** 6
nutritional count per serving 30.9g total fat (8g saturated fat); 559 cal; 26.8g carbohydrate; 40.9g protein; 4.7g fiber

old-fashioned lamb and celery root pie

2½ pounds diced lamb shoulder
½ cup plain (all-purpose) flour
2 tablespoons olive oil
1 large yellow onion, chopped
1 large carrot, chopped
1½ pounds celery root trimmed, chopped coarsely
1½ cups salt-reduced beef stock
2 teaspoons chopped fresh thyme
2 tablespoons chopped fresh flat-leaf parsley
1 egg, beaten lightly

SHORTCRUST PASTRY
1½ cups plain (all-purpose) flour
4 ounces butter, chopped coarsely
1 egg yolk
2 tablespoons iced water, approximately

1 Toss lamb in flour; shake away excess. Heat oil in large saucepan; cook lamb, in batches, until browned. Remove from pan.
2 Add onion, carrot and celery root to pan; cook, stirring, 5 minutes. Return lamb to pan with stock and herbs; simmer, covered, about 2 hours or until tender. Season to taste; cool.
3 Meanwhile, make shortcrust pastry.
4 Preheat oven to 350°F.
5 Spoon lamb mixture into 8-cup ovenproof dish; place on cookie sheet.
6 Roll pastry between sheets of parchment paper until large enough to cover top of dish. Brush edge of dish with egg. Place pastry over filling, trim edge; pinch edge in decorative pattern. Brush pastry with egg. Bake about 35 minutes or until browned.

SHORTCRUST PASTRY Process flour and butter until crumbly. Add egg yolk and most of the water; process until ingredients just come together. Knead pastry on floured surface until smooth, enclose with plastic wrap; refrigerate 1 hour.

prep + cook time 3 hours
(+ refrigeration & cooling) serves 6
nutritional count per serving 37.7g total fat
(18.4g saturated fat); 732 cal; 43g carbohydrate;
51.9g protein; 6.5g fiber

tip Ask the butcher for lamb shoulder, as what is sold as diced lamb is sometimes from the leg and will not be as tender.

curried beef and pea pie

1 tablespoon olive oil
1 large yellow onion, chopped finely
4 cloves garlic, crushed
1½ pounds ground beef
2 tablespoons curry powder
2 tablespoons plain (all-purpose) flour
2 tablespoons tomato paste
2 cups beef stock
¾ cup frozen peas
1 sheet puff pastry
1 egg, beaten lightly

1 Preheat oven to 425°F. Oil 6-cup ovenproof dish.
2 Heat oil in large saucepan; cook onion and garlic, stirring, until onion softens. Add beef; cook, stirring, until browned.

3 Add curry powder, cook, stirring, until fragrant. Add flour; cook, stirring, until mixture bubbles and thickens. Add paste; gradually stir in stock; stir until mixture boils and thickens; simmer, uncovered, 10 minutes. Stir in peas; season to taste.
4 Pour mixture into dish. Top with pastry; trim edge. Brush with egg; sprinkle with a little extra curry powder.
5 Bake about 20 minutes or until pastry is puffed and browned lightly.

prep + cook time 45 minutes **serves** 4
nutritional count per serving 27.2g total fat (7.4g saturated fat); 509 cal; 26.1g carbohydrate; 38.5g protein; 3.6g fiber

sausage, egg and bacon pies

3 bacon slices, halved
2 thick sausages
3 sheets shortcrust pastry
1 cup bottled tomato pasta sauce
6 eggs
2 scallions, sliced thinly

1 Preheat oven to 425°F. Oil six-hole (¾-cup) texas muffin pan.
2 Cook bacon in large frying pan until browned and crisp; drain on absorbent paper. Cook sausages in same pan until browned all over and cooked through; cool. Slice sausages thinly.

3 Cut two 5½-inch rounds from each pastry sheet; press rounds into pan holes. Prick bases with fork. Line bases and sides of each pan hole with bacon. Top with sausage; pour over sauce. Bake 10 minutes.
4 Using a spoon, make an indent in sauce. Crack an egg carefully into each pie; bake about 15 minutes or until egg is set.
5 Serve sprinkled with onion.

prep + cook time 50 minutes (+ cooling) **makes** 6
nutritional count per serving 45g total fat
(21.1g saturated fat); 681 cal; 41.6g carbohydrate;
26.7g protein; 3.8g fiber

moroccan-style lamb pies with harissa yogurt

2½ pounds diced lamb shoulder
½ cup plain (all-purpose) flour
2 tablespoons olive oil
2 medium yellow onions, chopped finely
2 medium carrots, chopped finely
2 cloves garlic, crushed
1 teaspoon each ground cilantro, cumin, ginger and turmeric
1 cinnamon stick
1½ cups beef stock
6 fresh dates, seeded, chopped coarsely
1 tablespoon honey
2 tablespoons finely chopped fresh cilantro
8 sheets filo pastry
1½ ounces butter, melted
2 teaspoons sesame seeds

HARISSA YOGURT
¾ cup thick yogurt
2 tablespoons harissa

1 Toss lamb in flour; shake away excess. Heat oil in large saucepan; cook lamb, in batches, until browned. Remove from pan.
2 Add onion and carrot to pan; cook, stirring, until soft. Add garlic and spices; cook, stirring, until fragrant. Return lamb to pan with stock; simmer, covered, 1½ hours.
3 Preheat oven to 425°F.
4 Simmer lamb, uncovered, about 30 minutes or until tender and sauce is thickened. Stir in dates, honey and cilantro; season to taste.
5 Spoon mixture into eight 1-cup ovenproof dishes. Brush each pastry sheet with butter, scrunch and place over filling. Sprinkle with seeds. Bake, uncovered, about 15 minutes or until browned.
6 Meanwhile, make harissa yogurt.
7 Serve pies with harissa yogurt.

HARISSA YOGURT Combine yogurt and half the harissa in small bowl. Serve topped with remaining harissa.

prep + cook time 3 hours 15 minutes (+ cooling)
serves 8
nutritional count per serving 22.2g total fat (10g saturated fat); 474 cal; 30.1g carbohydrate; 36.9g protein; 3.2g fiber

tip Ask the butcher for lamb shoulder, as what is sold as diced lamb is sometimes from the leg and will not be as tender.

note Harissa is a Tunisian hot chili paste, available in delicatessens and gourmet food stores. As every brand is different, add it gradually, a teaspoon at a time, until the desired heat is reached. We used a mild harissa.

mushroom and pancetta quiche

2 ounces butter
3 shallots, chopped finely
6½ ounces button mushrooms, sliced thickly
3 ounces swiss brown mushrooms, sliced thickly
2 cloves garlic, crushed
¾ cup sour cream
2 eggs
3 ounces thinly sliced pancetta

SHORTCRUST PASTRY
1½ cups plain (all-purpose) flour
4 ounces butter, chopped coarsely
1 egg yolk
2 tablespoons iced water, approximately

1 Make shortcrust pastry.
2 Roll pastry between sheets of parchment paper until large enough to line 11-inch loose-based tart pan. Lift pastry into pan; press into side, leaving edge overhanging slightly. Place pan on cookie sheet; refrigerate 30 minutes.
3 Meanwhile, preheat oven to 350°F.
4 Cover pastry with parchment paper, fill with dried beans or rice. Bake 15 minutes. Remove paper and beans; bake 15 minutes. Trim pastry edge with a sharp knife.
5 Heat butter in large frying pan. Add shallot; cook, stirring, until softened. Add mushrooms; cook, stirring, until softened. Stir in garlic; cook, stirring, until fragrant. Season to taste; cool.
6 Spoon mushroom mixture into pastry case. Combine sour cream and eggs in medium bowl; season. Pour egg mixture over mushrooms. Top with pancetta. Bake about 25 minutes or until set.

SHORTCRUST PASTRY Process flour and butter until crumbly. Add egg yolk and most of the water; process until ingredients just come together. Knead pastry on floured surface until smooth, enclose in plastic wrap; refrigerate 1 hour.

prep + cook time 1 hour 40 minutes
(+ refrigeration) **serves** 8
nutritional count per serving 32.8g total fat
(19.9g saturated fat); 424 cal; 22.1g carbohydrate;
10g protein; 2.2g fiber

penang pork curry pies

  1 tablespoon peanut oil
  ½ cup penang curry paste
  1 pound 2 ounces ground pork
  2 kaffir lime leaves, torn
1⅔ cups coconut milk
  ⅓ cup water
  2 tablespoons fish sauce
  ¼ cup grated palm sugar
5½ ounces green beans, chopped coarsely
  3 ounces broccoli, chopped finely
  1 small red pepper, chopped finely
  7 ounces canned bamboo shoots, drained
  ¼ cup coarsely chopped fresh cilantro
  2 sheets puff pastry
  1 egg, beaten lightly

1 Heat oil in large saucepan; add paste; cook, stirring, until fragrant. Add pork; cook, stirring, until changed in color. Stir in lime leaves, coconut milk, the water, sauce and sugar; bring to a boil. Simmer, uncovered, about 10 minutes or until reduced slightly.
2 Add beans, broccoli, pepper and bamboo shoots; simmer, uncovered, about 3 minutes or until vegetables are tender. Stir in cilantro. Discard lime leaves; cool.
3 Meanwhile, preheat oven to 425°F.
4 Spoon pork mixture into four 1½-cup ovenproof dishes.
5 Cut pastry a little larger than the tops of the dishes. Brush edge of dishes with egg. Place pastry over filling; place dishes on cookie sheet, brush with a little egg. Bake about 15 minutes or until pastry is browned and puffed.

prep + cook time 1 hour (+ cooling) **serves** 4
nutritional count per serving 57.5g total fat (24.2g saturated fat); 895 cal; 55.1g carbohydrate; 37.9g protein; 7.2g fiber

eggplant and hummus lamb tarts

¼ cup olive oil
2 tablespoons lemon juice
1 clove garlic, crushed
1 tablespoon finely chopped fresh flat-leaf parsley
1 tablespoon finely chopped fresh rosemary
1 pound lamb eye of loin
1 small eggplant, sliced thinly
1 tablespoon coarse cooking (kosher) salt
1 sheet puff pastry
1 egg, beaten lightly
1 tablespoon olive oil, extra
1½ ounces baby spinach leaves
¼ cup pitted small black olives

HUMMUS
¼ cup hot water
1½ tablespoons lemon juice
1 tablespoon olive oil
1 tablespoon tahini
1 clove garlic, chopped finely
1 teaspoon sea salt flakes
12½ ounces canned chickpeas, rinsed, drained

1 Combine oil with juice, garlic and herbs in pitcher; reserve ¼ cup marinade. Pour remaining mixture over lamb in shallow dish; turn to coat. Cover, refrigerate 2 hours.
2 Meanwhile, place eggplant in colander, sprinkle with salt. Stand eggplant 30 minutes. Rinse eggplant; pat dry.
3 Make hummus.
4 Preheat oven to 425°F.
5 Cut pastry in half. Place pastry on parchment-paper-lined cookie sheet. Prick pastry well with fork; brush pastry lightly with egg. Bake about 15 minutes or until puffed and browned.
6 Brush eggplant with extra oil; cook on heated oiled grill pan (or grill or barbecue) until browned on both sides and tender.
7 Season lamb, cook on grill pan until browned both sides and done as desired. Remove from pan; cover, stand 5 minutes before slicing thinly.
8 Spread hummus thickly over base of tarts, top with eggplant, lamb, spinach and olives; drizzle tarts with the reserved marinade.

HUMMUS Blend ingredients until smooth; season to taste.

prep + cook time 1 hour (+ refrigeration) serves 4
nutritional count per serving 44.6g total fat (7.1g saturated fat); 710 cal; 28.5g carbohydrate; 46.2g protein; 6.4g fiber

serving suggestion Serve with lemon wedges.

tip For a shortcut, use store-bought hummus and well-drained chargrilled eggplant.

moroccan lamb party pies

1 tablespoon vegetable oil
1 small yellow onion, chopped finely
1 clove garlic, crushed
14 ounces ground lamb
2 teaspoons ground cumin
1 cup undrained canned crushed tomatoes
¼ cup roasted pine nuts
2 tablespoons finely chopped raisins
2 tablespoons finely chopped fresh cilantro
3 sheets ready-rolled shortcrust pastry
1 egg, beaten lightly
2 sheets ready-rolled puff pastry

1 Heat oil in medium frying pan; cook onion and garlic, stirring, until onion softens. Add lamb; cook, stirring, until lamb changes color. Add cumin; cook, stirring, until fragrant. Add tomatoes; bring to the boil. Reduce heat; simmer, uncovered, about 5 minutes or until thickened slightly. Stir in nuts, raisins and cilantro; cool.
2 Preheat oven to 400°F. Grease two 12-hole (2-tablespoons deep) flat-based patty pans.
3 Cut twenty-four 3-inch rounds from shortcrust pastry; press into pan holes. Brush edges with a little of the egg. Spoon lamb mixture into pastry.
4 Cut twenty-four 2-inch rounds from puff pastry; top pies with puff pastry lids. Press edges firmly to seal; brush lids with egg. Cut a small slit in top of each pie.
5 Bake about 20 minutes or until browned lightly. Stand pies in pan 5 minutes before serving.

prep + cook time 1 hour **serves** 24
nutritional count per serving 12.2g total fat (5.5g saturated fat); 198 cal; 15.6g carbohydrate; 6.2g protein; 0.9g fiber

serving suggestion Accompany with mango chutney.

veal goulash pies

1½ pounds diced veal shoulder
2 tablespoons plain flour
1 tablespoon sweet paprika
¼ teaspoon cayenne pepper
¼ cup olive oil
1 small yellow onion, chopped finely
1 clove garlic, crushed
2 teaspoons caraway seeds
12½ ounces can diced tomatoes
¼ cup beef stock
1 medium red pepper, cut into ½ inch pieces
1 medium unpeeled potato, cut into
    ½ inch pieces
¼ cup sour cream
¼ cup coarsely chopped fresh flat-leaf parsley
2 sheets ready-rolled shortcrust pastry
1 egg, beaten lightly
2 sheets ready-rolled puff pastry

1 Coat veal in combined flour, paprika and pepper;
shake off excess. Heat 2 tablespoons of the oil in
large saucepan; cook veal, in batches, until browned.
2 Heat remaining oil in same pan; cook onion and
garlic, stirring, until onion softens. Return veal to
pan with seeds, undrained tomatoes and stock;
bring to the boil. Reduce heat; simmer, covered,
25 minutes. Add pepper and potato; simmer,
uncovered, about 15 minutes or until sauce
thickens. Stir in sour cream and parsley; cool.
3 Preheat oven to 400°F. Grease six-hole (¾-cup)
texas muffin pan.
4 Cut six 1-inch rounds from shortcrust pastry;
press into pan holes. Brush edges with a little of
the egg. Divide goulash among pastry cases.
5 Cut six 3-inch rounds from puff pastry; top
goulash with puff pastry rounds. Press edges firmly
to seal; brush tops with remaining egg. Cut a small
slit in top of each pie.
6 Bake about 25 minutes. Stand pies in pan 5
minutes before serving, top-side up.

prep + cook time 1 hour 40 minutes serves 6
nutritional count per serving 44.6g total fat
(19.7g saturated fat); 765 cal; 56g carbohydrate;
33.3g protein; 4.1g fiber

vegetable pies

vegetable and lentil potato pie

½ cup french-style green lentils
1 tablespoon olive oil
1 medium yellow onion, chopped finely
1 medium carrot, chopped coarsely
2 stalks celery, trimmed, chopped coarsely
1 medium parsnip, chopped coarsely
2 cloves garlic, crushed
6½ ounces button mushrooms, sliced thickly
2 bay leaves
1 tablespoon finely chopped fresh rosemary
¼ cup tomato paste
1 cup vegetable stock
13 ounces canned diced tomatoes
4½ ounces green beans, trimmed, chopped coarsely
9½ ounces potatoes, chopped coarsely
9½ ounces sweet potato, chopped coarsely
2 ounces butter
½ cup finely grated parmesan cheese

1 Cook lentils in large saucepan of boiling water until tender; drain.

2 Meanwhile, heat oil in large saucepan; cook onion, carrot, celery, parsnip and garlic, stirring, until vegetables soften. Add mushrooms, bay leaves and rosemary; cook, stirring, until fragrant. Stir in paste, stock and undrained tomatoes; bring to a boil. Reduce heat; simmer, uncovered, about 20 minutes or until thickened. Add beans and lentils; cook, stirring, about 3 minutes or until beans are tender. Season to taste.

3 Meanwhile, boil, steam or microwave potato and sweet potato, separately, until tender; drain. Mash potato with half the butter until smooth; season to taste. Mash sweet potato with remaining butter until smooth; season to taste.

4 Preheat oven to 400°F.

5 Spoon lentil mixture into 8-cup ovenproof dish. Top with potato mash. Swirl through sweet potato mash; sprinkle with cheese. Bake, uncovered, about 30 minutes or until cheese is browned.

prep + cook time 1 hour 15 minutes **serves** 6
nutritional count per serving 14.5g total fat
(7.3g saturated fat); 310 cal; 28.4g carbohydrate;
12.8g protein; 8.7g fiber

caramelized leek and brie tartlets

1 tablespoon olive oil
2 tablespoons butter
2 medium leeks, sliced finely
1 clove garlic, crushed
1 tablespoon brown sugar
1 tablespoon white wine vinegar
3 sheets ready-rolled puff pastry
7 ounce piece brie cheese
24 sprigs lemon thyme

1 Preheat oven to 375°F. Grease two 12-hole deep tart pans.
2 Heat oil and butter in large frying pan; cook leek over medium heat, stirring, about 5 minutes or until leek softens. Add garlic, sugar and vinegar; cook, stirring, about 8 minutes or until leek caramelizes.
3 Cut 8 squares from each pastry sheet; press one pastry square into each pan hole. Divide leek mixture among pastry cases.
4 Cut cheese into 24 slices. Place a slice of cheese and thyme sprig on top of each tartlet. Bake about 20 minutes.

prep + cook time 40 minutes **serves** 24
nutritional count per serving 8.8g total fat (4.8g saturated fat); 128 cal; 8.7g carbohydrate; 3.1g protein; 0.8g fiber

tip To make the squares, we used a 3¼ inch square cutter, measuring 3¼ inch from corner to corner.

feta and spinach filo bundles

1½ cups spinach, trimmed
1 tablespoon olive oil
1 medium yellow onion, chopped finely
2 cloves garlic, crushed
½ teaspoon ground nutmeg
5 ounces feta cheese, crumbled
3 eggs
2 teaspoons finely grated lemon rind
¼ cup coarsely chopped fresh mint
2 tablespoons finely chopped fresh dill
6 tablespoons butter, melted
6 sheets filo pastry

1 Boil, steam or microwave spinach until wilted; drain. Refresh in cold water; drain. Squeeze out excess moisture. Chop spinach coarsely; spread out on paper towels.

2 Heat oil in small frying pan; cook onion and garlic, stirring, until onion softens. Add nutmeg; cook, stirring, until fragrant. Cool. Combine onion mixture and spinach in medium bowl with cheese, eggs, rind and herbs.

3 Preheat oven to 375°F. Brush six-hole (¾-cup) texas muffin pan with a little of the butter.

4 Brush each sheet of filo with melted butter; fold in half to enclose buttered side. Gently press one sheet into each pan hole.

5 Divide spinach mixture among filo-lined muffin holes; fold filo over filling to enclose. Brush with butter. Bake about 15 minutes. Turn filo bundles out, top-side up, onto parchment-paper-lined cookie sheet; bake about 5 minutes or until browned lightly. Stand 5 minutes before serving, top-side up.

prep + cook time 45 minutes **makes** 6
nutritional count per serving 22.9g total fat (12.3g saturated fat); 287 cal; 9.6g carbohydrate; 10.4g protein; 1.8g fiber

baked cheesy polenta with salsa

2 cups chicken stock
2 cups water
1 cup polenta
½ cup mozzarella cheese
3½ ounces feta cheese, crumbled

SALSA
2 medium avocados, chopped coarsely
⅔ cup drained sun-dried tomatoes in oil, chopped coarsely
1 cucumber, chopped coarsely
1 small red pepper, chopped coarsely
⅓ cup coarsely chopped fresh flat-leaf parsley
½ teaspoon dried chili flakes
¼ cup red wine vinegar
¼ cup olive oil

1 Grease 12-hole (⅓-cup) muffin pan.
2 Bring stock and the water to the boil in medium saucepan; gradually stir in polenta. Reduce heat; simmer, stirring, about 10 minutes or until polenta thickens. Stir in cheeses. Spoon polenta into muffin pan; smooth tops. Refrigerate 1 hour.
3 Preheat oven to 425°F.
4 Bake polenta for 15 minutes. Gently turn polenta onto parchment-paper-lined cookie sheet; bake about 5 minutes or until browned lightly.
5 Meanwhile, make salsa by combining ingredients in medium bowl.
6 Serve warm polenta, top-side up, topped with salsa.

prep + cook time 45 minutes (+ refrigeration time)
serves 12
nutritional count per serving 15.2g total fat (4.2g saturated fat); 219 cal; 13.7g carbohydrate; 6g protein; 2.4g fiber

tip For a vegetarian option use vegetable stock.

roast sweet potato and spinach frittata

2 medium sweet potatoes
1 tablespoon olive oil
2 teaspoons ground cumin
1 cup baby spinach leaves, chopped coarsely
¼ cup finely grated parmesan cheese
6 eggs, beaten lightly
⅔ cup cream

1 Preheat oven to 350°F. Grease six-hole (¾-cup) texas muffin pan; line with parchment paper.
2 Peel sweet potatoes; cut into slices. Combine sweet potato, oil and cumin in large, shallow baking dish; roast about 20 minutes or until tender. Cool 10 minutes.
3 Divide spinach, cheese then sweet potato among muffin pan holes, finishing with sweet potato.
4 Whisk egg and cream in medium bowl; pour into pan holes.
5 Bake about 25 minutes. Stand in pan 5 minutes; using a small knife, loosen frittata from edge of pan before turning out, top-side up.

prep + cook time 1 hour **makes** 6
nutritional count per serving 21g total fat (10.3g saturated fat); 303 cal; 16.9g carbohydrate; 10.8g protein; 2.3g fiber

olive and roasted tomato tart

8 ounces cherry tomatoes, halved
¼ cup pesto dip
4 eggs
¾ cup light cream
1 small red onion, sliced thinly
⅓ cup pitted black olives, halved
⅓ cup ricotta cheese, crumbled
¾ ounce arugula leaves

SHORTCRUST PASTRY
1½ cups plain (all-purpose) flour
4 ounces cold butter, chopped coarsely
1 egg yolk
1 tablespoon iced water, approximately

1 Make shortcrust pastry.
2 Preheat oven to 350°F. Line cookie sheet with parchment paper.
3 Place tomatoes, cut-side up, on tray. Bake about 20 minutes or until tender.
4 Oil 9½-inch round tart pan. Roll pastry between sheets of parchment paper until large enough to line pan. Lift pastry into pan; press into side, trim edge, prick base all over with fork. Refrigerate 20 minutes.
5 Increase oven to 400°F. Place pan on cookie sheet; cover pastry with parchment paper, fill with dried beans or rice. Bake 10 minutes. Remove paper and beans; bake 5 minutes; cool.
6 Reduce oven to 350°F.
7 Spread pastry with pesto dip. Whisk eggs and cream in large bowl; season. Place tomatoes over dip, pour egg mixture over them. Top with onion, olives and cheese. Bake about 45 minutes or until set. Top with arugula.

SHORTCRUST PASTRY Process flour and butter until crumbly. Add egg yolk and most of the water; process until ingredients just come together. Enclose in plastic wrap; refrigerate 30 minutes.

prep + cook time 1 hour 40 minutes (+ refrigeration) **serves** 6
nutritional count per serving 40.9g total fat (23.2g saturated fat); 549 cal; 32.3g carbohydrate; 12.7g protein; 2.7g fiber

double-crust pizza

1 medium yellow onion, sliced thinly
1 large zucchini, sliced thinly
1 medium red pepper, sliced thinly
2 cloves garlic, crushed
½ cup sun-dried tomato strips
½ cup pitted black olives, halved
9 ounces artichokes in brine, drained, halved
½ cup tomato paste
1 cup coarsely grated mozzarella cheese
1 egg, beaten lightly

PIZZA DOUGH
2 cups plain (all-purpose) flour
1½ teaspoons dry yeast
½ teaspoon salt
¾ cup water
2 tablespoons olive oil

1 Make pizza dough.
2 Meanwhile, heat remaining oil in large frying pan; cook onion, zucchini, pepper and garlic, stirring, until vegetables are tender. Remove from heat; add tomato, olives and artichokes.
3 Preheat oven to 400°F. Oil cookie sheet.
4 Turn dough onto floured surface; divide in half. Roll one portion to a 12-inch round. Transfer to sheet. Spread tomato paste over base, top with filling, leaving a ¾-inch border. Sprinkle with cheese; brush edge with a little egg. Roll remaining dough to a 12-inch round. Cover filling with dough, press edges to seal. Brush with egg.
5 Cut three slashes in center of pie. Bake about 30 minutes or until browned. Stand 5 minutes.

PIZZA DOUGH Place flour, yeast and salt in large bowl; gradually stir in the water and half the oil, mix to a soft dough. Knead dough on floured surface about 5 minutes or until elastic; place in large oiled bowl, turn once to coat in oil. Cover; stand in a warm place about 1 hour or until dough doubles.

prep + cook time 1 hour (+ standing) serves 6
nutritional count per serving 12.3g total fat (3.7g saturated fat); 385 cal; 49.1g carbohydrate; 15.3g protein; 7g fiber

spinach and three cheese muffins

2 tablespoons olive oil
1 small yellow onion, chopped finely
3½ ounces baby spinach leaves
½ cup coarsely grated mozzarella cheese
½ cup coarsely grated parmesan cheese
3½ ounces blue cheese, crumbled
1 quantity basic muffin mix *(see pizza muffins recipe, page 57)*

1 Preheat oven to 400°F. Grease 12-hole (⅓-cup) muffin pan.
2 Heat oil in medium frying pan; cook onion, stirring, until onion softens. Add spinach; cook, stirring, about 1 minute or until wilted. Cool.
3 Combine cheeses and spinach mixture in large bowl with basic muffin mix. Do not over-mix; mixture should be lumpy.
4 Divide mixture among pan holes. Bake about 20 minutes. Stand muffins 5 minutes before turning, top-side up, onto wire rack. Serve muffins warm.

prep + cook time 45 minutes **serves** 12
nutritional count per serving 14.6g total fat (7.5g saturated fat); 241 cal; 17.1g carbohydrate; 8.9g protein; 3.1g fiber

pumpkin and feta muffins

1 tablespoon olive oil
7 ounce piece pumpkin, cut into ½ inch pieces
1 clove garlic, crushed
2 ounces feta cheese, crumbled
¼ cup finely grated parmesan cheese
¼ cup finely chopped fresh chives
1 quantity basic muffin mix (see pizza muffins recipe, page 57)

1 Preheat oven to 400°F. Grease 12-hole (⅓-cup) muffin pan.
2 Heat oil in small frying pan; cook pumpkin, stirring, about 5 minutes or until tender. Add garlic; cook, stirring, 1 minute. Cool.
3 Combine cheeses, chives and pumpkin mixture in medium bowl with basic muffin mix. Do not over-mix; mixture should be lumpy.
4 Divide mixture among pan holes. Bake about 20 minutes. Stand muffins 5 minutes before turning, top-side up, onto wire rack. Serve muffins warm.

prep + cook time 45 minutes makes 12
nutritional count per serving 10g total fat
(5.3g saturated fat); 192 cal; 7.7g carbohydrate;
6.3g protein; 3.1g fiber

serving suggestion Accompany warm muffins with butter.

roasted garlicky squash and sage pies

1¾ pounds butternut squash, chopped coarsely
4 cloves garlic, unpeeled
1 tablespoon olive oil
3 eggs, beaten lightly
½ cup light cream
¼ cup coarsely chopped fresh sage
2½ ounces feta cheese
1½ tablespoons pine nuts

SPICY PASTRY
1½ cups plain (all-purpose) flour
1 teaspoon ground cilantro
1 teaspoon cumin seeds
4 ounces cold butter, chopped coarsely
1 egg yolk
2 tablespoons ice water, approximately

1 Preheat oven to 425°F.
2 Place squash and garlic on parchment-paper-lined cookie sheet, drizzle with oil. Bake about 20 minutes or until tender. Transfer to large bowl; cool 5 minutes. Squeeze garlic from skins. Mash squash and garlic coarsely with a fork. Stir in eggs, cream and sage; season.
3 Meanwhile, make spicy pastry.
4 Grease six 3½-inch x 5-inch oval pie pans. Divide pastry into six even pieces. Roll each piece between sheets of parchment paper until large enough to line pans. Lift pastry into pans; press into side, trim edge. Refrigerate 20 minutes.
5 Reduce oven to 400°F. Place pans on cookie sheet; cover pastry with parchment paper, fill with dried beans or rice. Bake 10 minutes. Remove paper and beans; bake about 5 minutes or until browned lightly. Cool.
6 Fill pastry cases with squash mixture. Sprinkle with crumbled cheese and nuts. Bake about 35 minutes or until set and browned.

SPICY PASTRY Process flour, spices and butter until crumbly. Add egg yolk and most of the water; process until ingredients just come together. Enclose pastry in plastic wrap; refrigerate 30 minutes.

prep + cook time 1 hour 30 minutes
(+ refrigeration) makes 6
nutritional count per serving 40g total fat
(21.3g saturated fat); 563 cal; 36.2g carbohydrate;
14g protein; 3.5g fiber

butternut squash and goat cheese lasagne

1½ pound butternut squash, peeled
1 tablespoon olive oil
3 fresh lasagne sheets
6 ounces baby spinach leaves
4¼ ounces goat cheese, chopped finely
¼ cup finely grated parmesan cheese

WHITE SAUCE
¼ cup butter
1 tablespoon plain (all-purpose) flour
1½ cups milk
¼ cup finely grated parmesan cheese

1 Preheat oven to 400°F. Grease six-hole (¾-cup) texas muffin pan; line each muffin hole with two criss-crossed 2 x 8 inch strips of parchment paper.
2 Cut squash lengthwise into ½-inch-thick slices. Cut six 2¾-inch rounds and six 3¼-inch rounds from squash slices. Brush pumpkin rounds with oil; place in large baking dish in a single layer. Roast about 15 minutes or until tender.
3 Meanwhile, cut six 2¾-inch rounds and twelve 3¼-inch rounds from lasagne sheets.
4 Make white sauce.
5 Boil, steam or microwave spinach until wilted; drain. Refresh in cold water; drain. Squeeze out excess moisture. Chop spinach coarsely; spread out on paper towels.
6 Divide a third of the white sauce among muffin holes; place one small pasta round in each hole; top with half the goat cheese, half the spinach then a small squash round. Repeat layers with another third of the sauce, six large pasta rounds and remaining goat cheese, spinach and squash. Top lasagne stacks with remaining pasta rounds and white sauce; sprinkle with parmesan.
7 Bake about 25 minutes or until browned lightly. Let stand in pan 5 minutes. Using parchment paper strips as lifters, carefully remove lasagne from muffin holes. Serve top-side up.

WHITE SAUCE Melt butter in medium saucepan, add flour; cook, stirring, 1 minute. Gradually stir in milk; cook, stirring, until sauce boils and thickens. Stir in cheese.

prep + cook time 1 hour 10 minutes **makes** 6
nutritional count per serving 14.1g total fat (7.6g saturated fat); 243 cal; 17g carbohydrate; 11.1g protein; 2.3g fiber

four-bean chili pie with cornbread crust

1	tablespoon olive oil
1	medium yellow onion, chopped finely
1	medium green pepper, chopped finely
2	cloves garlic, crushed
2	teaspoons chili powder
1	teaspoon ground cumin
1½	pounds canned diced tomatoes
1½	cups vegetable stock
12½	ounces canned cranberry beans, rinsed, drained
12½	ounces canned black beans, rinsed, drained
12½	ounces canned red kidney beans, rinsed, drained
12½	ounces canned cannellini beans, rinsed, drained
¼	cup finely chopped fresh cilantro
¾	cup self-raising flour
¾	cup polenta
3	ounces butter, chopped coarsely
1	egg, beaten lightly
⅓	cup coarsely grated cheddar cheese
4	ounces canned corn kernels, drained
2	tablespoons milk, approximately

1 Heat oil in large saucepan; cook onion, green pepper and garlic, stirring, until onion softens. Add chili and cumin; cook, stirring, until fragrant. Add undrained tomatoes, stock and beans; bring to a boil. Reduce heat; simmer, uncovered, about 15 minutes or until sauce has thickened slightly. Stir in cilantro; season to taste.

2 Meanwhile, preheat oven to 400°F. Place flour and polenta in medium bowl; rub in butter. Stir in egg, cheese, corn and enough milk to make a soft, sticky dough.

3 Spoon bean mixture into 8-cup ovenproof dish. Drop level tablespoons of dough mixture on top of bean mixture. Bake, uncovered, about 20 minutes or until browned.

prep + cook time 1 hour **serves** 6
nutritional count per serving 21.2g total fat (10.8g saturated fat); 561 cal; 62.9g carbohydrate; 21.4g protein; 15.7g fiber

quiche primavera

5½ ounces asparagus, trimmed, halved
2 ounces green beans, trimmed, halved lengthwise
¼ cup frozen peas
4 eggs
½ cup light cream
½ cup sour cream
1 small zucchini, sliced into ribbons
1 scallion, sliced thinly
¼ cup small fresh mint leaves

SHORTCRUST PASTRY
1½ cups plain (all-purpose) flour
4 ounces cold butter, chopped coarsely
1 egg yolk
2 tablespoons ice water, approximately

1 Make shortcrust pastry.
2 Oil 9½-inch round tart pan. Roll pastry between sheets of parchment paper until large enough to line pan. Lift pastry into pan; press into side, trim edge. Refrigerate 20 minutes.
3 Preheat oven to 400°F.
4 Place pan on cookie sheet; cover pastry with parchment paper, fill with dried beans or rice. Bake 10 minutes. Remove paper and beans; bake 5 minutes or until browned lightly. Cool. Reduce oven to 350°F.
5 Meanwhile, boil, steam or microwave asparagus, beans and peas, separately, until just tender; drain. Refresh under cold water.
6 Whisk eggs, cream and sour cream together in large bowl; season. Arrange asparagus, beans, peas and zucchini in cooled pastry; sprinkle with onion. Pour over egg mixture. Bake about 45 minutes or until just set. Sprinkle with mint leaves.

SHORTCRUST PASTRY Blend or process flour and butter until crumbly. Add egg yolk and most of the water; process until ingredients just come together. Enclose in plastic wrap; refrigerate 30 minutes.

prep + cook time 1 hour 45 minutes (+ refrigeration) serves 6
nutritional count per serving 30.1g total fat (23.9g saturated fat); 518 cal; 30g carbohydrate; 11.5g protein; 2.8g fiber

spiced green pea and potato pasties

1 tablespoon olive oil
2 medium yellow onions, sliced thinly
1 tablespoon superfine sugar
1 tablespoon moroccan seasoning
2 cloves garlic, crushed
1 teaspoon fresh thyme leaves
1 medium potato, chopped coarsely
11 ounces butternut squash, chopped coarsely
⅔ cup frozen peas
5 sheets pre-made pie crusts
1 egg, beaten lightly
2 teaspoons sesame seeds

1 Heat oil in large frying pan; cook onion and sugar, stirring, about 15 minutes or until caramelized. Stir in seasoning, garlic and thyme. Cook, stirring, until fragrant; transfer to large bowl.
2 Meanwhile, boil, steam or microwave potato and squash, separately, until tender; drain. Add potato, squash and peas to bowl. Stir gently to combine; season to taste, cool.
3 Preheat oven to 400°F. Line cookie sheet with parchment paper.
4 Cut ten 5¼-inch rounds from pastry. Spoon ⅓ cup potato mixture on each round; brush edges with egg. Bring pastry edges together to form a semi-circle. Pinch edges together to seal.
5 Place pasties on trays. Brush with egg; sprinkle with seeds. Bake about 30 minutes or until browned lightly.

prep + cook time 1 hour (+ cooling) **makes** 10
nutritional count per serving 25.7g total fat
(12.6g saturated fat); 447 cal; 45g carbohydrate;
8g protein; 3.1g fiber

tip Unrolled pre-made pie crusts are available in the dairy section of most supermarkets.

huevos rancheros

6 6-inch corn tortillas
14 ounce can kidney beans, rinsed, drained
½ cup bottled chunky tomato salsa
1 small tomato, chopped coarsely
2 tablespoons coarsely chopped fresh cilantro
6 eggs
½ cup coarsely grated cheddar cheese
1 small avocado, chopped coarsely
1 tablespoon lime juice

1 Preheat oven to 400°F. Grease six-hole (¾-cup) texas muffin pan.
2 Soften tortillas according to manufacturer's instructions. Gently press one tortilla into each muffin hole to form a cup.
3 Combine beans, salsa, tomato and cilantro in small bowl; divide half the bean mixture among tortilla cups. Break one egg into each cup. Sprinkle with cheese.
4 Bake about 12 minutes or until eggs are cooked.

5 Meanwhile, stir avocado and juice into remaining bean mixture.
6 Serve huevos rancheros topped with avocado mixture.

prep + cook time 17 minutes **serves** 6
nutritional count per serving 14.5g total fat (5g saturated fat); 230 cal; 11.8g carbohydrate; 12.1g protein; 2.8g fiber

serving suggestion Sour cream and lime wedges.

mini vegetable curry pies

1 tablespoon vegetable oil
2 scallions, sliced thinly
1 medium red pepper, chopped finely
1 medium potato, chopped finely
1 medium zucchini, chopped finely
1 medium carrot, chopped finely
⅓ cup mild curry paste
2 cups vegetable stock
4 ounces canned corn kernels, drained
½ cup frozen peas
3 sheets pre-made pie crusts
2 sheets puff pastry
1 egg, beaten lightly
1 teaspoon cracked black pepper

1 Heat oil in large frying pan; cook onion, red pepper, potato, zucchini and carrot, stirring, until softened. Stir in paste, cook until fragrant. Add stock; bring to a boil. Reduce heat to medium, simmer, uncovered, until potato is tender and stock evaporated. Stir in corn and peas, remove from heat; season to taste. Cool.
2 Preheat oven to 400°F. Oil a 12-hole (⅓-cup) muffin pan. Cut twelve 3½-inch rounds from pre-made pie crusts. Line muffin holes with pastry. Fill with vegetable mixture. Cut twelve 3-inch rounds from puff pastry. Brush one side of rounds with egg. Place rounds, egg side down over filling; press edges to seal. Brush tops with egg. Sprinkle with pepper.
3 Bake pies about 30 minutes or until browned. Stand 5 minutes before serving.

prep + cook time 1 hour 10 minutes **makes** 12
nutritional count per serving 22.3g total fat (7.1g saturated fat); 372 cal; 34.6g carbohydrate; 7g protein; 3.2g fiber

tip Unrolled pre-made pie crusts are available in the dairy section of most supermarkets.

onion and smoked cheddar tarts

  1 tablespoon olive oil
  2 large yellow onions, sliced thinly
  4 eggs
  ¾ cup light cream
  ⅔ cup finely grated smoked cheddar cheese
1½ teaspoons fresh thyme leaves

PARMESAN PASTRY
1½ cups plain (all-purpose) flour
  ⅓ cup finely grated parmesan cheese
  3 ounces cold butter, chopped coarsely
  1 egg yolk
  2 tablespoons iced water, approximately

1 Make parmesan pastry.
2 Oil six 3½-inch round tart pans. Divide pastry into six even pieces. Roll each piece of pastry between sheets of parchment paper until large enough to line pans. Lift pastry into pans; press into side, trim edge. Cover; refrigerate 20 minutes.
3 Preheat oven to 400°F.
4 Place pans on cookie sheet, cover pastry with parchment paper, fill with dried beans or rice. Bake 10 minutes. Remove paper and beans; bake about 5 minutes or until browned lightly, cool.
5 Meanwhile, heat oil in large frying pan; cook onion, stirring, about 15 minutes or until caramelized. Remove from heat.
6 Whisk eggs and cream together in large bowl; season. Place onion on top of pastry. Pour in egg mixture; sprinkle with cheese and thyme. Bake about 25 minutes or until set.

PARMESAN PASTRY Blend or process flour, cheese and butter until crumbly. Add egg yolk and most of the water; process until ingredients just come together. Enclose pastry in plastic wrap; refrigerate 30 minutes.

prep + cook time 1 hour 20 minutes
(+ refrigeration) **makes** 6
nutritional count per serving 40.5g total fat
(23.2g saturated fat); 553 cal; 31.7g carbohydrate;
15.6g protein; 2.3g fiber

goat cheese and zucchini flower quiche

12 baby zucchini with flowers
 3 sheets ready-rolled shortcrust pastry
 3 ounces firm goat cheese, chopped finely
⅓ cup finely grated parmesan cheese
 2 tablespoons finely chopped garlic chives
 1 quantity quiche filling *(see crab, fennel and herb quiche recipe, page 108)*

1 Preheat oven to 400°F. Grease 12-hole (⅓-cup) muffin pan.
2 Remove flowers from zucchini; remove and discard stamens from flowers. Slice zucchini thinly.
3 Cut twelve 3-inch rounds from pastry; press into pan holes. Divide combined sliced zucchini, cheeses and chives into pastry; pour quiche filling into pastry cases. Top each quiche with a zucchini flower.
4 Bake about 25 minutes. Stand in pan 5 minutes before serving.

prep + cook time 50 minutes **makes** 12
nutritional count per serving 25.8g total fat (15g saturated fat); 340 cal; 19.9g carbohydrate; 7.1g protein; 1.1g fiber

roasted pepper and goat cheese terrine

   3 large red peppers
1½ cups ricotta cheese, chopped coarsely
   8 ounces firm goat cheese, chopped coarsely
   ¼ cup finely chopped fresh chives
   2 tablespoons lemon juice
   1 clove garlic, crushed

SPINACH AND WALNUT PESTO
   ¼ cup finely grated parmesan cheese
3½ ounces baby spinach leaves
   ¼ cup roasted walnuts
   1 clove garlic, quartered
   ¼ cup olive oil
   2 tablespoons lemon juice
   1 tablespoon water

1 Preheat oven to 450°F. Grease six holes of eight-hole (½-cup) petite loaf pan. Line base and two long sides of each hole with a strip of parchment paper, extending 2 inches over sides.
2 Halve peppers; discard seeds and membranes. Place on oven tray; roast, skin-side up, about 15 minutes or until skin blisters and blackens. Cover with plastic wrap for 5 minutes then peel away skin. Cut pepper into strips; line base and two long sides of pan holes with pepper strips, extending ½ inch over edges.
3 Combine remaining ingredients in medium bowl; spoon cheese mixture into pan holes, pressing down firmly. Fold pepper strips over to enclose filling. Cover; refrigerate 1 hour.
4 Meanwhile, make spinach and walnut pesto.
5 Carefully remove terrines from pan holes; serve with spinach and walnut pesto; sprinkle with chopped fresh chives.

SPINACH AND WALNUT PESTO Process cheese, spinach, nuts and garlic until chopped finely. With motor operating, gradually add combined oil, juice and the water in a thin, steady stream; process until pesto is smooth.

prep + cook time 45 minutes (+ refrigeration)
makes 6
nutritional count per serving 26.8g total fat (10.8g saturated fat); 339 cal; 7.5g carbohydrate; 16.5g protein; 2.6g fiber

feta and spinach filo bundles

12 ounces spinach, trimmed
1 tablespoon olive oil
1 medium yellow onion, chopped finely
2 cloves garlic, crushed
½ teaspoon ground nutmeg
5 ounces feta cheese, crumbled
3 eggs
2 teaspoons finely grated lemon rind
¼ cup coarsely chopped fresh mint
2 tablespoons finely chopped fresh dill
3 ounces butter, melted
6 sheets filo pastry

1 Boil, steam or microwave spinach until soft; drain. Refresh in cold water; drain. Squeeze out excess moisture. Chop spinach coarsely; spread out on paper towel.
2 Heat oil in small frying pan; cook onion and garlic, stirring, until onion softens. Add nutmeg; cook, stirring, until fragrant. Cool. Combine onion mixture and spinach in medium bowl with cheese, eggs, rind and herbs.
3 Preheat oven to 400°F. Brush six-hole (¾-cup) texas muffin pan with a little of the butter.
4 Brush each sheet of filo with melted butter; fold in half to enclose buttered side. Gently press one sheet into each pan hole.
5 Divide spinach mixture among pastry; fold filo over filling to enclose. Brush with butter. Bake about 15 minutes. Turn filo bundles out, top-side up, onto parchment-paper-lined oven tray; bake about 5 minutes or until browned lightly. Stand 5 minutes before serving, top-side up.

prep + cook time 45 minutes **makes** 6
nutritional count per serving 22.9g total fat (12.3g saturated fat); 287 cal; 9.6g carbohydrate; 10.4g protein; 1.8g fiber

sun-dried tomato and asparagus tart

8 ounces asparagus, trimmed, halved
2 sheets shortcrust pastry
3 eggs
⅓ cup light cream
⅓ cup finely grated pecorino cheese
½ cup sun-dried tomatoes in oil, drained, sliced thinly
2 ounces feta cheese, crumbled
1 teaspoon fresh thyme leaves

1 Boil, steam or microwave asparagus until tender; drain. Refresh under cold water; drain.
2 Line base and sides of 4½-inch x 13½-inch rectangular loose-based flan pan with pastry, joining pastry where needed. Trim excess. Place pan in freezer 20 minutes.
3 Preheat oven to 400°F.
4 Place pan on oven tray. Line pastry with parchment paper. Fill with dried beans or rice. Bake 10 minutes. Remove beans and paper. Bake about 5 minutes or until browned lightly; cool 5 minutes. Reduce oven to 350°F.
5 Whisk eggs, cream and pecorino together in large mixing bowl; season. Place asparagus into pastry. Pour over egg mixture. Top with tomato, feta and thyme. Bake about 25 minutes or until set.

prep + cook time 1 hour 5 minutes (+ freezing)
makes 10
nutritional count per serving 41.6g total fat (22.5g saturated fat); 636 cal; 45.1g carbohydrate; 18.8g protein; 5.2g fiber

tip You can use one quantity of shortcrust pastry, page 6, instead of the store-bought sheets.

seafood pies

tomato and saffron fish pies

1 cup fish stock
1 bay leaf
pinch saffron threads
1 tablespoon olive oil
1 medium red onion, chopped finely
3 cloves garlic, crushed
1 long fresh red chili, sliced thinly
1 medium red pepper, chopped coarsely
13 ounces canned crushed tomatoes
1¼ pounds firm white fish fillets, chopped coarsely
2 tablespoons coarsely chopped fresh
   flat-leaf parsley
1 thin french bread stick, sliced thickly
cooking-oil spray

1 Combine stock, bay leaf and saffron in medium saucepan. Bring to a boil; simmer, covered, 5 minutes.
2 Preheat oven to 425°F. Oil six 1-cup ovenproof dishes.
3 Meanwhile, heat oil in large saucepan; cook onion, garlic, chili and pepper, stirring, until vegetables are tender. Add undrained tomatoes and hot stock mixture. Bring to a boil; simmer, uncovered, about 10 minutes or until thickened slightly. Remove from heat, stir in fish and parsley; season. Divide mixture among dishes; place on oven tray. Top each dish with two or three slices of bread. Spray bread with oil.
4 Bake uncovered, about 15 minutes or until bread is crisp.

prep + cook time 40 minutes **makes** 6
nutritional count per serving 7g total fat
(1.4g saturated fat); 249 cal; 18.5g carbohydrate;
26.3g protein; 2.8g fiber

note We used ling in this recipe, but any white fish fillet will be fine.

greek shrimp pies

1 tablespoon olive oil
1 medium yellow onion, chopped finely
2 cloves garlic, crushed
3 teaspoons plain (all-purpose) flour
¼ cup dry white wine
13 ounces canned diced tomatoes
1½ pounds uncooked medium shrimp, shelled, deveined
2 tablespoons finely chopped fresh flat-leaf parsley
12 sheets filo pastry
2 ounces butter, melted
1½ ounces feta cheese, crumbled

1 Heat oil in large frying pan; cook onion and garlic, stirring, until onion softens. Add flour, cook; stirring 1 minute. Add wine and undrained tomatoes; bring to a boil, stirring. Reduce heat; simmer, uncovered, about 3 minutes or until sauce thickens slightly. Add shrimp and parsley; cook 1 minute. Season to taste. Cool.
2 Preheat oven to 400°F. Oil six-hole (¾-cup) texas muffin pan.
3 Layer two sheets of pastry, brushing each with butter. Fold in thirds to enclose buttered side. Brush with butter; fold in half, forming a square; brush with butter. Gently press into muffin hole. Repeat with remaining pastry and butter.
4 Bake pastry about 5 minutes or until browned lightly.
5 Divide shrimp mixture among pastry; top with cheese. Bake about 10 minutes or until browned lightly. Stand 5 minutes before serving.

prep + cook time 45 minutes (+ cooling) **makes** 6
nutritional count per serving 14.4g total fat (7.3g saturated fat); 300 cal; 21.3g carbohydrate; 18.5g protein; 2.2g fiber

serving suggestion Serve with lemon wedges.

smoked cod and cheddar pie

    1 pound smoked cod
2⅓ cups milk
    1 bay leaf
    1 ounce butter
    1 medium yellow onion, chopped finely
6½ ounces ham, chopped finely
    2 tablespoons plain (all-purpose) flour
    ⅓ cup dry white wine
    ½ cup coarsely grated cheddar cheese
    2 tablespoons finely chopped fresh chives
12½ ounces white fish fillets, chopped coarsely
    1 sheet puff pastry
    1 egg, beaten lightly

1 Preheat oven to 425°F. Oil 6-cup ovenproof dish.
2 Place cod in large saucepan with 1⅓ cups of
the milk and bay leaf. Bring to a boil; simmer,
uncovered, 5 minutes. Drain; discard milk and bay
leaf. Flake fish; discard skin and bones.
3 Heat butter in same pan; cook onion and ham,
stirring, until onion is soft. Add flour; cook, stirring,
until mixture bubbles and thickens. Gradually add
wine; simmer, uncovered, 1 minute. Gradually stir
in remaining milk; simmer, uncovered, 1 minute;
remove from heat. Stir in cheese, chives and all
fish; season.
4 Spoon mixture into dish. Top with pastry,
trimming to fit. Use pastry scraps to decorate pie.
Brush pastry with egg. Bake about 20 minutes or
until browned.

prep + cook time 40 minutes **serves** 4
nutritional count per serving 38.2g total fat
(15.9g saturated fat); 747 cal; 28.3g carbohydrate;
69.2g protein; 1.3g fiber

tip We used ling in this recipe, but any firm white
fish fillet will be fine.

crab, fennel and herb quiche

3 sheets ready-rolled shortcrust pastry
1 tablespoon olive oil
1 medium fennel bulb, sliced thinly
8 ounces crab meat
2 tablespoons finely chopped fennel fronds
2 tablespoons finely chopped fresh flat-leaf parsley
½ cup coarsely grated cheddar cheese

QUICHE FILLING
1¼ cup cream
¼ cup milk
3 eggs

1 Preheat oven to 400°F. Grease 12-hole (⅓-cup) muffin pan.
2 Cut twelve 3½-inch rounds from pastry; press into muffin holes.
3 Heat oil in large frying pan; cook fennel, stirring, about 5 minutes or until fennel softens and browns slightly. Divide fennel among pastry; top with combined crab, fronds, parsley and cheese.
4 Make quiche filling.
5 Pour quiche filling into pastry. Bake about 25 minutes. Stand in pan 5 minutes before serving with lime wedges.

QUICHE FILLING Whisk ingredients in large jug.

prep + cook time 50 minutes **makes** 12
nutritional count per serving 27.1g total fat (15g saturated fat); 361 cal; 20.3g carbohydrate; 9g protein; 1.3g fiber

tips We used lump crab meat from the fish market. Reserve fennel fronds when slicing the bulb.

creamy bacon and fish pie with potato topping

2 ounces butter
2 bacon slices, sliced thinly
1 medium leek, trimmed, sliced thinly
2 tablespoons plain (all-purpose) flour
¾ cup chicken stock
1 cup light cream
3 cups broccoli florets
1¼ pounds skinless white fish fillets, chopped coarsely
1 medium potato, sliced thinly
¼ cup coarsely grated cheddar cheese

1 Preheat oven to 425°F. Oil 6-cup ovenproof dish.
2 Melt butter in large saucepan; cook bacon and leek, stirring, until leek is soft. Add flour; cook, stirring, until mixture bubbles and thickens. Gradually stir in stock, cream and broccoli. Stir over heat until mixture boils and thickens. Add fish; stir until heated through. Season

3 Spoon mixture into dish. Top with potato, sprinkle with cheese.
4 Bake uncovered, about 25 minutes or until browned lightly.

prep + cook time 45 minutes (+ cooling) serves 4
nutritional count per serving 45.2g total fat (27.3g saturated fat); 666 cal; 14.3g carbohydrate; 49.2g protein; 5g fiber

note We used blue eye in this recipe, but any white fish fillet will be fine.

curry shrimp and roti pies

2 tablespoons vegetable oil
1 medium yellow onion, chopped coarsely
½ -inch piece fresh ginger, grated
⅓ cup curry paste
¾ cup chicken stock
5 large plum tomatoes, chopped coarsely
1½ pounds uncooked shrimp, shelled, deveined
½ cup frozen peas
¼ cup coarsely chopped fresh cilantro
4 roti bread

1 Preheat oven to 425°F. Oil four 1¼-cup ovenproof dishes.

2 Heat half the oil in large frying pan; cook onion and ginger; stirring, until onion softens. Add paste; cook, stirring, until fragrant. Add stock and tomato; bring to a boil, simmer, uncovered, about 5 minutes or until tomato is tender. Remove from heat. Stir in shrimp, peas and cilantro; season. Spoon mixture into dishes.
3 Cut two 3½-inch rounds from each roti bread. Place over filling. Brush with remaining oil. Bake pies, uncovered, about 15 minutes or until browned and crisp.

prep + cook time 45 minutes **makes** 4
nutritional count per serving 20.6g total fat (2.9g saturated fat); 464 cal; 35.9g carbohydrate; 29.6g protein; 8.3g fiber

note You can purchase roti bread at Indian food stores or substitute flatbread.

fish pies with potato topping

2 medium potatoes
1½ ounces butter
1 small leek, sliced thinly
¼ cup plain (all-purpose) flour
1 cup light cream
1 pound thick white boneless fish fillets, chopped coarsely
2 tablespoons finely chopped fresh flat-leaf parsley
¾ ounce butter, melted, extra

PASTRY
1½ cups plain (all-purpose) flour
2½ ounces butter
1 egg
2 tablespoons ice water, approximately

1 Make pastry.
2 Boil or steam whole unpeeled potatoes about 20 minutes or until tender. Drain; cool. Peel potatoes; slice thinly.
3 Meanwhile, melt butter in medium saucepan; cook leek, stirring, until soft. Add flour; cook, stirring, 1 minute. Gradually stir in cream; stir over heat until mixture boils and thickens. Season to taste, cool. Stir in fish and parsley.
4 Preheat oven to 400°F. Oil six 1-cup ovenproof dishes. Roll pastry between sheets of parchment paper until large enough to line dishes. Lift pastry into dishes, ease into bases and sides; trim edges. Prick bases well; place dishes on cookie sheet. Refrigerate 30 minutes.
5 Bake pastry 15 minutes. Cool.
6 Spoon fish mixture into pastry. Top with slightly overlapping potato slices; brush with extra butter. Bake about 20 minutes or until browned. Stand pies 5 minutes before serving.

PASTRY Process flour and butter until crumbly. Add egg and most of the water; process until ingredients just come together. Knead pastry on floured surface until smooth, enclose with plastic wrap; refrigerate 30 minutes.

prep + cook time 1 hour 15 minutes
(+ refrigeration & cooling) **makes** 6
nutritional count per serving 38g total fat
(23.7g saturated fat); 592 cal; 37g carbohydrate;
24.9g protein; 2.7g fiber

serving suggestion Serve with lemon wedges.

tip We used blue eye in this recipe, but any firm white fish fillet will be fine.

smoked salmon vol-au-vents

2 sheets puff pastry
1 egg, beaten lightly
4 ounces smoked salmon, chopped finely
1 cucumber, seeded, chopped finely
½ small red onion, chopped finely
1 tablespoon baby capers, chopped finely
1 tablespoon finely chopped fresh dill
1 tablespoon lime juice
2 tablespoons sour cream

1 Preheat oven to 400°F. Line a cookie sheet with parchment paper.
2 Cut twelve 3¼-inch rounds from pastry; place on cookie sheet. Brush edges of pastry rounds with egg. Cut out 3½-inch rounds from center of six of the rounds; place rings onto rounds. Brush with egg.
3 Bake pastry about 12 minutes or until browned lightly. Gently press center of cases with a tea towel to flatten.
4 Combine salmon, cucumber, onion, capers, dill and juice in medium bowl; season to taste. Spoon into pastry. Top with sour cream.

prep + cook time 30 minutes **makes** 6
nutritional count per serving 23.5g total fat (3.6g saturated fat); 382 cal; 31.1g carbohydrate; 10.9g protein; 1.4g fiber

thai-flavored scallop pies

12 wonton or gow gee wrappers
¼ cup vegetable oil
3 shallots, chopped finely
1 fresh small serrano chili,
    chopped finely
⅔ cup coconut milk
1 tablespoon fish sauce
1 tablespoon lime juice
3 teaspoons light brown sugar
3 fresh kaffir lime leaves, shredded finely
3 teaspoons cornstarch
1 tablespoon water
1 pound scallops, without roe, chopped coarsely
¼ cup fresh cilantro leaves
1 fresh small serrano chili, sliced thinly, extra

1 Preheat oven to 400°F. Oil 12-hole (⅓-cup) muffin pan.
2 Brush wrappers with half the oil; press into muffin holes. Bake about 10 minutes or until crisp. Stand in pan 5 minutes. Transfer to a wire rack; cool.
3 Heat remaining oil in large frying pan; cook shallot and chili, stirring, until softened. Add coconut milk, sauce, juice, sugar and lime leaves. Cook, stirring, until fragrant. Bring to a boil. Stir in cornstarch and the water; cook, stirring, until sauce boils and thickens.
4 Add scallops; simmer, uncovered, until almost cooked through. Season. Spoon scallop mixture into pie shells. Top with cilantro and extra chili.

prep + cook time 30 minutes makes 12
nutritional count per serving 7.8g total fat
(3.1g saturated fat); 116 cal; 5.5g carbohydrate;
5.9g protein; 0.5g fiber

salmon coulibiac

    1 cup cooked white rice
    2 scallions, sliced thinly
    2 hard-boiled eggs, mashed
    1 tablespoon mayonnaise
    1 tablespoon finely chopped fresh dill
6½ ounces canned red salmon, drained
    1 egg, beaten lightly

SHORTCRUST PASTRY
    2 cups plain (all-purpose) flour
    8 ounces cold butter, chopped
    1 teaspoon finely grated lemon rind
    ¼ cup ice water, approximately

1 Make shortcrust pastry.
2 Preheat oven to 425°F. Heat large cookie sheet.
3 Combine rice and onion in small bowl. Combine egg, mayonnaise and dill in small bowl; season. Remove skin and bones from salmon; mash.
4 Cut one third of pastry from block; refrigerate. Roll remaining pastry between sheets of parchment paper until 8 inches x 10½ inches.
5 Spoon rice mixture over pastry, leaving a 1¼-inch border. Top with salmon then egg mixture.
6 Roll refrigerated pastry until 9½ inches x 11½ inches. Mark a rectangle ¾-inch in from edge of pastry. Put pastry over filling, pressing edges together. Mark lines across pastry. Brush with egg.
7 Bake on cookie sheet about 20 minutes or until browned. Stand 5 minutes.

SHORTCRUST PASTRY Pulse flour, butter and rind five times in processor; turn onto flat surface. Knead in enough of the water until pastry just comes together. Enclose in plastic wrap; refrigerate 30 minutes.

prep + cook time 1 hour (+ refrigeration) serves 6 nutritional count per serving 41.8g total fat (24.5g saturated fat); 614 cal; 43.7g carbohydrate; 15.7g protein; 2.1g fiber

tuna, pasta and chargrilled vegetable pie

    8 ounces penne pasta
    3 medium zucchini, sliced thinly
    1 medium red pepper, quartered
    3 baby eggplants, sliced thinly
    2 tablespoons olive oil
    1 medium yellow onion, chopped finely
    2 cloves garlic, crushed
   13 ounces canned crushed tomatoes
 13½ ounces canned tuna in oil, drained, flaked
    2 tablespoons finely chopped fresh basil
    4 eggs, beaten lightly
    1 cup coarse breadcrumbs
    ¼ cup mozzarella cheese

1 Cook pasta in medium saucepan of boiling water, uncovered, until tender; drain.

2 Meanwhile, combine zucchini, pepper and eggplant in large bowl with half the oil; season. Cook vegetables on heated oiled grill plate (or grill, barbecue or grill pan) until browned both sides and tender. Cut into small pieces.

3 Preheat oven to 400°F. Oil 9-inch springform tin; line base and side with parchment paper. Stand tin on oven tray.

4 Heat remaining oil in large saucepan; cook onion and garlic, stirring, until tender. Add undrained tomatoes; bring to a boil. Simmer, uncovered, 2 minutes. Remove from heat, stir in tuna, basil, vegetables and pasta; season to taste. Cool slightly; stir in eggs. Pour mixture into tin. Sprinkle with breadcrumbs and cheese.

5 Bake pie about 50 minutes or until browned and set. Stand 20 minutes before serving.

prep + cook time 1 hour 25 minutes (+ standing)
serves 8
nutritional count per serving 14.5g total fat (2.8g saturated fat); 341 cal; 29.8g carbohydrate; 20.7g protein; 3.7g fiber

tip Pie is best left to cool completely before slicing.

salmon and potato soufflés

 2 medium potatoes, chopped coarsely
10 ounce salmon fillets
 2 tablespoons packaged breadcrumbs
¼ cup butter
 1 small yellow onion, chopped finely
 2 tablespoons plain flour
¾ cup milk
 2 egg yolks
 3 eggs whites
¼ cup finely grated parmesan cheese
 2 tablespoons finely chopped garlic chives
 1 teaspoon finely grated lemon rind

1 Boil, steam or microwave potato until tender; drain. Mash until smooth.
2 Meanwhile, cook fish in medium saucepan of simmering water, uncovered, about 4 minutes or until cooked. When cool enough to handle, flake fish.
3 Preheat oven to 400°F. Grease six-hole (¾-cup) texas muffin pan.
4 Divide breadcrumbs among pan holes; shake pan to coat bases and sides with breadcrumbs. Place pan on oven tray.
5 Melt butter in medium saucepan; cook onion, stirring, until onion softens. Add flour; cook, stirring, until mixture thickens and bubbles. Gradually stir in milk; cook, stirring, until mixture boils and thickens. Transfer mixture to large bowl; stir in egg yolks, cheese, chives, rind, potato and salmon.
6 Beat egg whites in small bowl with electric mixer until soft peaks form. Fold egg whites into salmon mixture, in two batches. Divide soufflé mixture among pan holes. Bake about 20 minutes.
7 Gently turn soufflés out; serve immediately, top-side up.

prep + cook time 45 minutes **makes** 6
nutritional count per serving 14.7g total fat (7.4g saturated fat); 250 cal; 12.2g carbohydrate; 16.9g protein; 1.1g fiber

serving suggestion Accompany with lemon wedges and sour cream.

fish chowder pies

1½ ounce butter
1 medium yellow onion, chopped coarsely
1 clove garlic, crushed
3 bacon slices, chopped coarsely
2 tablespoons plain flour
1 cup milk
½ cup cream
2 small potatoes, cut into ½-inch pieces
1¼ pounds firm white fish fillets, cut into
 ¾-inch pieces
¼ cup finely chopped fresh chives
2 sheets ready-rolled shortcrust pastry
1 egg, beaten lightly
2 sheets ready-rolled puff pastry

1 Melt butter in large saucepan; cook onion, garlic and bacon, stirring, until onion softens.
2 Add flour; cook, stirring, 1 minute. Gradually stir in combined milk and cream; bring to the boil. Add potato; simmer, covered, stirring occasionally, 8 minutes. Add fish; simmer, uncovered, 2 minutes; cool. Stir in chives.
3 Preheat oven to 400°F. Grease six-hole (¾-cup) texas muffin pan.
4 Cut six 4½-inch rounds from shortcrust pastry; press into pan holes. Brush edges with a little of the egg. Divide fish chowder among pastry cases.
5 Cut six 3½-inch rounds from puff pastry; top chowder with puff pastry rounds. Press edges firmly to seal; brush tops with remaining egg. Cut a small slit in top of each pie.
6 Bake about 25 minutes. Stand pies in pan 5 minutes before serving, top-side up, sprinkled with chopped fresh chives.

prep + cook time 1 hour 5 minutes **makes** 6
nutritional count per serving 51.5g total fat (28g saturated fat); 842 cal; 60g carbohydrate; 37.9g protein; 2.9g fiber

sweet pies & tarts

white chocolate and raspberry trifles

½ jam-filled sponge roll
¼ cup sweet sherry
14 ounce can peach halves in natural juice, drained
 2 tablespoons custard powder
 2 tablespoons superfine sugar
½ cup cream
½ cup milk
 1 vanilla bean
4½ ounces white eating chocolate, chopped coarsely
 3 ounces packet raspberry gelatin
 1 cup frozen raspberries

1 Line each hole of a six-hole (¾-cup) texas muffin pan with plastic wrap. Cut sponge roll into six ⅜-inch-thick slices; cut 2½-inch rounds from each slice, discard remainder. Place one round in each pan hole; brush with sherry. Place one peach half, cut-side down, in each pan hole; gently press peaches to flatten slightly.
2 Combine custard powder and sugar in small saucepan; gradually stir in cream and milk. Split vanilla bean in half lengthwise; scrape seeds into pan (reserve pod for another use). Cook, stirring, until mixture boils and thickens. Remove from heat; stir in chocolate until smooth.
3 Pour custard into pan holes; smooth surface. Refrigerate 30 minutes.
4 Meanwhile, make gelatin according to manufacturer's instructions; refrigerate until gelatin is set to the consistency of unbeaten egg white.
5 Sprinkle berries over custard; spoon gelatin over berries; refrigerate 3 hours or overnight.
6 Turn onto serving plates, top side-down, gently remove plastic wrap.

prep + cook time 35 minutes (+ refrigeration) **serves** 6
nutritional count per serving 19.2g total fat (12g saturated fat); 458 cal; 61.6g carbohydrate; 5.8g protein; 2.4g fiber

serving suggestion Serve accompanied by fresh raspberries.

baklava figs

6 sheets filo pastry
1¾ ounces butter, melted
12 large fresh figs
⅓ cup firmly packed brown sugar
1 teaspoon mixed spice
½ teaspoon ground cinnamon
2¾ ounces butter, chopped coarsely
½ cup finely chopped roasted walnuts
¼ cup slivered almonds
1 teaspoon finely grated orange rind

MAPLE CREAM
10½ ounces heavy cream
2 tablespoons maple syrup

1 Preheat oven to 400°F. Grease 12-hole (⅓-cup) muffin pan.
2 Brush three pastry sheets with melted butter; stack together. Repeat with remaining pastry. Cut each pastry stack into six rectangles (you will have 12 rectangles). Gently press one stack into each muffin hole.
3 Quarter each fig, cutting three-quarters of the way down the fig. Place one fig in each pastry.
4 Combine sugar and spices in medium bowl; using fingers, rub in chopped butter. Stir in nuts and rind; gently push mixture into the center of figs. Bake about 15 minutes.
5 Meanwhile, make maple cream.
6 Serve baklava figs, dusted with a little sifted icing sugar, and maple cream.

MAPLE CREAM Beat cream and syrup in small bowl with electric mixer until soft peaks form.

prep + cook time 35 minutes serves 12
nutritional count per serving 23.7g total fat (12.3g saturated fat); 313 cal; 20.5g carbohydrate; 3.7g protein; 2.7g fiber

white chocolate and raspberry bread puddings

3 small croissants
3½ ounces white chocolate, chopped coarsely
1 cup fresh raspberries
1¼ cups milk
¾ cup cream
2 tablespoons superfine sugar
½ teaspoon vanilla extract
3 eggs

1 Preheat oven to 315°F. Grease six-hole (¾-cup) texas muffin pan; line each muffin hole with two criss-crossed 2 inch x 8 inch strips of parchment paper.
2 Split each croissant in half lengthwise then tear each half into pieces. Roughly line each muffin hole with croissant pieces. Sprinkle with chocolate and berries.
3 Combine milk, cream, sugar and extract in small saucepan; bring to a boil. Whisk eggs in large bowl; gradually whisk in hot milk mixture. Pour custard into muffin holes.
4 Place pan in large baking dish; add enough boiling water to come halfway up sides of pan. Bake about 35 minutes or until puddings set. Remove pan from dish; stand puddings 15 minutes. Using parchment paper strips, lift puddings from muffin holes onto serving plates. Serve dusted with a little sifted confectioners' sugar.

prep + cook time 1 hour (+ standing) serves 6
nutritional count per serving 29.2g total fat
(17.4g saturated fat); 421 cal; 29.7g carbohydrate;
9.6g protein; 2.1g fiber

serving suggestion Serve accompanied by fresh raspberries.

variation
dark chocolate and fig bread pudding
Omit the white chocolate and replace with
3½ ounces coarsely chopped dark chocolate.
Omit the raspberries and replace with 2 coarsely
chopped fresh large figs.

blood orange meringue pies

½ cup superfine sugar
2 tablespoons cornstarch
⅔ cup blood orange juice
2 tablespoons water
2 teaspoons finely grated blood orange rind
2½ ounces unsalted butter, chopped coarsely
2 eggs, separated
½ cup superfine sugar, extra

PASTRY
1¼ cups plain (all-purpose) flour
¼ cup superfine sugar
4½ ounces cold butter, chopped coarsely
1 egg yolk

1 Make pastry.
2 Grease 12-hole (⅓-cup) muffin pan. Roll pastry between sheets of parchment paper to ½-inch thickness; cut out twelve 3¼-inch rounds. Press rounds into muffin holes; prick bases all over with fork. Refrigerate 30 minutes.
3 Preheat oven to 400°F.
4 Bake pastry 10 minutes. Cool.
5 Meanwhile, combine sugar and cornstarch in small saucepan; gradually stir in juice and the water until smooth. Cook, stirring, until mixture boils and thickens. Reduce heat; simmer, stirring, 1 minute. Remove from heat; stir in rind, butter and egg yolks. Cool 10 minutes.
6 Divide filling among pastry. Refrigerate 1 hour.
7 Increase temperature to 475°F.
8 Beat egg whites in small bowl with electric mixer until soft peaks form; gradually add extra sugar, beating until sugar dissolves.
9 Roughen surface of filling with fork; using star nozzle, pipe meringue over filling. Bake about 3 minutes or until browned lightly.

PASTRY Process flour, sugar and butter until coarse. Add egg yolk; process until combined. Knead on lightly floured surface until smooth. Cover; refrigerate 30 minutes.

prep + cook time 50 minutes
(+ refrigeration and cooling time) serves 12
nutritional count per serving 15.3g total fat
(9.5g saturated fat); 299 cal; 36.7g carbohydrate;
3.2g protein; 0.6g fiber

tip If pastry is too dry, add 2 teaspoons of water with the egg yolk.

variation
lemon meringue tarts Increase the sugar in filling to ⅔ cup. Omit orange rind and replace with 2 teaspoons finely grated lemon rind. Omit orange juice and replace with ⅔ cup lemon juice.

white chocolate, lime and ginger mousse tarts

3 ounces white chocolate, chopped coarsely
1 egg yolk
3 teaspoons finely grated lime rind
⅔ cup heavy cream, whipped

GINGER PASTRY
1½ cups plain (all-purpose) flour
2 tablespoons confectioners' sugar
1 teaspoon ground ginger
4 ounces cold butter, chopped coarsely
1 egg yolk
2 tablespoons iced water, approximately

1 Make ginger pastry. Grease ten 3¼-inch round loose-based flan pans.
2 Divide pastry into 10 portions, roll each between sheets of parchment paper until large enough to line pans. Lift pastry into pans. Press into sides; trim edges. Prick bases with fork, place on oven trays. Refrigerate 20 minutes.
3 Meanwhile, preheat oven to 400°F.
4 Bake pastry 20 minutes. Cool.
5 Melt chocolate in medium heatproof bowl over medium saucepan of simmering water. Cool 10 minutes. Stir in egg yolk and rind; fold in cream.
6 Spoon chocolate mousse mixture into pastry. Refrigerate 2 hours or until firm.

GINGER PASTRY Process flour, confectioners' sugar, ginger and butter until crumbly. Add egg yolk and enough of the water to make ingredients just come together. Knead dough on floured surface until smooth. Enclose with plastic wrap; refrigerate 30 minutes.

prep + cook time 45 minutes
(+ refrigeration & cooling) **makes** 10
nutritional count per serving 20.5g total fat (12.9g saturated fat); 297 cal; 23.9g carbohydrate; 4.5g protein; 0.9g fiber

passionfruit curd and coconut tarts

1 cup dried coconut
1 egg white, beaten lightly
2 tablespoons superfine sugar
¼ cup heavy cream, whipped
1 tablespoon passionfruit pulp

PASSIONFRUIT CURD
½ cup passionfruit pulp
½ teaspoon finely grated lemon rind
1 tablespoon lemon juice
½ cup superfine sugar
2½ ounces butter, chopped coarsely
1 egg, beaten lightly
1 egg yolk

1 Make passionfruit curd.
2 Preheat oven to 300°F. Grease 12-hole
(2-tablespoon) mini muffin pan.
3 Combine coconut, egg white and sugar in bowl.
Press mixture firmly and evenly over bases and
sides of pan holes. Bake about 20 minutes or until
browned lightly. Cool.
4 Fold cream into ½ cup of the passionfruit curd.
Reserve remaining curd for another use.
5 Divide passionfruit mixture among coconut
cases; top each with a little passionfruit pulp.

PASSIONFRUIT CURD Press passionfruit firmly
through a sieve over a small bowl. You will need
¼ cup passionfruit juice for this recipe. Combine
passionfruit juice with remaining ingredients in
medium heatproof bowl. Stir over a medium
saucepan of simmering water until the mixture
thickly coats the back of a wooden spoon, about
10 minutes. Cool; refrigerate 2 hours or until cold.

prep + cook time 1 hour 15 minutes
(+ cooling & refrigeration) **makes** 12
nutritional count per serving 12.6g total fat
(8.6g saturated fat); 178 cal; 13.4g carbohydrate;
2.1g protein; 2.7g fiber

tips You will need about six passionfruit for this
recipe. Remaining passionfruit curd is delicious on
scones, in pavlovas or meringues.

whiskey-laced mince pies

⅓ cup raisins, chopped finely
¼ cup golden raisins, chopped finely
¼ cup currants
1 small apple, grated coarsely
⅓ cup whiskey
⅓ cup light brown sugar
1 teaspoon finely grated lemon rind
1 teaspoon ground cinnamon
1½ ounces frozen butter, grated coarsely
1 egg, beaten lightly
2 tablespoons light brown sugar, extra

CINNAMON PASTRY
1½ cups plain (all-purpose) flour
½ teaspoon ground cinnamon
4 ounces butter, chopped coarsely
1 egg

1 To make fruit mince, combine dried fruit, apple, whiskey, sugar, rind and cinnamon in medium bowl. Cover; stand 48 hours. Stir in butter.
2 Make cinnamon pastry.
3 Preheat oven to 350°F. Grease 15 holes of two 12-hole (2 tablespoon) deep flat-based tart pans. Roll pastry between sheets of parchment paper until large enough to line pans. Cut fifteen 2½-inch rounds from pastry. Line pan holes with pastry, barely fill with fruit mince.
4 Cut fifteen 2¼-inch rounds from pastry. Cut small rounds from centers of each round. Place over filling, press edges together. Brush pies with egg; sprinkle with extra sugar.
5 Bake pies about 30 minutes. Stand 5 minutes before transferring to a wire rack to cool.

CINNAMON PASTRY Process flour, cinnamon and butter until crumbly. Add egg; process until ingredients just come together. Knead dough on floured surface. Enclose with plastic wrap; refrigerate 30 minutes.

prep + cook time 1 hour
(+ standing & refrigeration) **makes** 15
nutritional count per serving 10g total fat
(6.2g saturated fat); 200 cal; 24.9g carbohydrate;
2.8g protein; 1.1g fiber

pear and cinnamon sugar lattice pies

3 large pears, peeled, cored, sliced thinly
¼ cup superfine sugar
2 teaspoons cornstarch
1 teaspoon vanilla extract
1 egg white
½ teaspoon ground cinnamon

PASTRY
1½ cups plain (all-purpose) flour
2 tablespoons confectioners' sugar
4 ounces cold butter, chopped coarsely
1 egg yolk
2 tablespoons iced water, approximately

1 Make pastry.
2 Grease four 4-inch round loose-based flan pans.
Divide pastry into five portions. Roll each of four
portions between parchment paper until large
enough to line pans. Lift pastry into pans, press
into sides; trim edges. Reserve pastry scraps with
the fifth portion. Refrigerate 30 minutes.
3 Preheat oven to 350°F.
4 Meanwhile, combine pear and one-third of the
sugar in medium saucepan. Cook, covered, until
pear is tender. Drain, reserve 1 tablespoon liquid.
Blend or process mixture until almost smooth.
Return to pan with half the remaining sugar. Blend
cornstarch with reserved liquid; stir into pear
mixture; stir over heat until mixture boils and
thickens. Stir in extract; cool.
5 Spoon pear filling into pastry. Brush edges with
egg white. Roll all reserved pastry between sheets
of parchment paper. Cut into twelve ½-inch strips.
Weave strips over pies. Trim edges, pressing to
seal; sprinkle with combined remaining sugar and
cinnamon. Bake about 50 minutes.

PASTRY Process flour, confectioners' sugar and
butter until crumbly. Add egg yolk and enough of
the water to make ingredients just come together.
Knead dough on floured surface until smooth.
Enclose in plastic wrap; refrigerate 30 minutes.

prep + cook time 1 hour 15 minutes (+ refrigeration)
makes 4
nutritional count per serving 27.9g total fat
(17.5g saturated fat); 574 cal; 86.1g carbohydrate;
8.5g protein; 5.6g fiber

apple and mixed berry filo pie

6 medium apples, peeled, cored,
    sliced thinly
¼ cup superfine sugar
2 teaspoons cornstarch
2 teaspoons water
2 teaspoons vanilla extract
½ teaspoon ground cinnamon
9½ ounces frozen mixed berries
4 sheets filo pastry
1 ounce butter, melted
¼ teaspoon ground cinnamon, extra
2 tablespoons slivered almonds

1 Preheat oven to 425°F. Grease 4-cup pie dish.
2 Combine apple and sugar in large saucepan. Bring to the boil; simmer, covered, about 8 minutes or until tender.
3 Blend cornstarch with the water in small mixing bowl, stir into apple mixture with extract and cinnamon; stir gently over heat until mixture boils and thickens slightly. Stir in berries, spoon into dish.
4 Brush each sheet of pastry with butter. Scrunch and place over filling. Sprinkle with extra cinnamon and nuts.
5 Bake pie about 20 minutes until browned.

prep + cook time 45 minutes **serves** 6
nutritional count per serving 6.4g total fat
(2.9g saturated fat); 163 cal; 31.7g carbohydrate;
2.7g protein; 5.6g fiber

spiced apple parcels

1½ ounces butter
3 medium apples, peeled, cored, chopped finely
2 tablespoons maple syrup
1 tablespoon superfine sugar
½ teaspoon mixed spice
¼ cup golden raisins
¼ cup slivered almonds, toasted
1½ sheets butter puff pastry
1 egg, beaten lightly

1 Melt butter in large frying pan; cook apple, stirring occasionally, about 5 minutes or until browned lightly. Add maple syrup, sugar and spice; cook, stirring, about 5 minutes or until liquid boils and caramelizes. Transfer to medium heatproof bowl. Stir in golden raisins and nuts. Cool 20 minutes.

2 Meanwhile, preheat oven to 425°F.
3 Cut whole pastry sheet in quarters; cut half sheet in half. Spoon ¼ cup apple mixture along one half of pastry squares. Fold over to form rectangles, pressing edges to seal with a fork. Brush with egg. Make three slits in parcels.
4 Bake about 20 minutes or until browned.

prep + cook time 45 minutes (+ cooling) **makes** 6
nutritional count per serving 20.5g total fat (10.1g saturated fat); 346 cal; 35.4g carbohydrate; 5g protein; 2.4g fiber

serving suggestion Dust with sifted confectioners' sugar and serve with ice cream.

berry and rhubarb pies

2 cups coarsely chopped rhubarb
¼ cup superfine sugar
2 tablespoons water
1 tablespoon cornstarch
2 cups frozen mixed berries
1 egg white
2 teaspoons superfine sugar, extra

PASTRY
1⅔ cups plain (all-purpose) flour
⅓ cup superfine sugar
5½ ounces cold butter, chopped coarsely
1 egg yolk

1 Make pastry.
2 Place rhubarb, sugar and half the water in medium saucepan; bring to a boil. Reduce heat; simmer, covered, about 3 minutes or until rhubarb is tender. Blend cornstarch with the remaining water; stir into rhubarb mixture. Stir over heat until mixture boils and thickens. Remove from heat; stir in berries. Cool.
3 Grease six-hole (¾-cup) texas muffin pan. Roll two-thirds of the pastry between sheets of parchment paper to ⅛-inch thickness; cut out six 4½-inch rounds. Press rounds into muffin holes. Refrigerate 30 minutes.
4 Preheat oven to 400°F.
5 Roll remaining pastry between sheets of parchment paper to ⅛-inch thickness; cut out six 3½-inch rounds.
6 Divide fruit mixture among pastry cases.
7 Brush edge of 3½-inch rounds with egg white; place over filling. Press edges firmly to seal. Brush tops with egg white; sprinkle with extra sugar. Bake about 30 minutes.
8 Stand pies in pan 10 minutes; using palette knife, loosen pies from edge of pan before lifting out. Serve warm.

PASTRY Process flour, sugar and butter until coarse. Add egg yolk; process until combined. Knead on floured surface until smooth. Cover; refrigerate 30 minutes.

prep + cook time 1 hour 5 minutes
(+ refrigeration time) makes 6
nutritional count per serving 22.1g total fat
(13.9g saturated fat); 464 cal; 57.1g carbohydrate;
7.2g protein; 3.9g fiber

serving suggestion Serve with vanilla ice cream.

tips You need four large stems of rhubarb to get the required amount of chopped rhubarb. If pastry is too dry, add 2 teaspoons of water with the egg yolk.

variation
apple and blackberry pies Omit rhubarb and replace with 2 peeled, coarsely chopped medium apples. Cook with sugar and the water for about 5 minutes or until apples are just tender. Omit mixed berries and replace with 5½ ounces blackberries.

french apple quince tarts

1 sheet butter puff pastry
1½ ounces quince paste
2 tablespoons water
2 small apples, peeled

1 Preheat oven to 400°F. Line large oven tray with parchment paper.
2 Cut four 4½-inch rounds from pastry; place on tray about 1 inch apart. Heat paste with the water in small saucepan until smooth. Brush pastry with some of the quince mixture.

3 Quarter and core apples; slice thinly. Overlap slices on pastry. Brush apple with a little more quince mixture. Bake about 20 minutes or until pastry is crisp and apple is tender.
4 Brush tarts with remaining quince mixture; serve tarts warm.

prep + cook time 40 minutes **serves** 4
nutritional count per serving 9.5g total fat (5.1g saturated fat); 191 cal; 23.1g carbohydrate; 2.5g protein; 2.1g fiber

serving suggestion Serve with vanilla ice cream.

tip Choose small apples – golden delicious or granny smith are best so they will fit on the small pastry rounds neatly.

rhubarb pies with meringue topping

1 bunch fresh rhubarb, trimmed
1 tablespoon superfine sugar
2 sheets pre-made pie crusts
2 egg whites
½ cup superfine sugar, extra
1 tablespoon slivered almonds, chopped coarsely

1 Preheat oven to 400°F. Grease 12-hole (1½-tablespoon) shallow round-based patty pans.
2 Chop rhubarb into ¾-inch cubes. Spread rhubarb onto parchment-paper-lined oven tray; sprinkle with sugar. Bake, uncovered, about 10 minutes or until tender; cool.
3 Cut 12 2½-inch rounds from pastry. Press rounds into muffin holes; prick bases with fork. Refrigerate 20 minutes.
4 Bake pastry 10 minutes; cool.
5 Beat egg whites in small bowl with electric mixer until soft peaks form; gradually add extra sugar, beating until sugar dissolves.
6 Divide rhubarb filling among pastry. Spoon meringue over filling; sprinkle with nuts. Bake about 5 minutes or until browned lightly. Stand 5 minutes before serving.

prep + cook time 55 minutes
(+ cooling & refrigeration) **makes** 12
nutritional count per serving 9.1g total fat
(4.1g saturated fat); 190 cal; 23.5g carbohydrate;
3.3g protein; 1.4g fiber

tip Unrolled pre-made pie crusts are available in the dairy section of most supermarkets.

chocolate, peanut and caramel cheesecakes

12 chocolate wafer cookies
1 teaspoon gelatin
1 tablespoon water
9 ounces cream cheese, softened
⅓ cup superfine sugar
¾ cup cream
2 x 2 ounce Snickers bars, chopped finely
¼ cup crushed nuts
3½ ounces milk chocolate, chopped coarsely
2 tablespoons cream, extra

1 Line each hole of a greased six-hole (¾-cup) texas muffin pan with plastic wrap. Chop cookies into ½-inch pieces; divide among muffin holes.
2 Sprinkle gelatin over the water in small heatproof pitcher. Stand pitcher in small saucepan of simmering water; stir until gelatin dissolves, cool 5 minutes.
3 Beat cream cheese and sugar in small bowl with electric mixer until smooth; beat in cream until combined. Stir in gelatin mixture, chocolate bar and nuts.
4 Divide mixture among muffin holes; smooth surface. Refrigerate overnight.
5 Combine chocolate and extra cream in small saucepan; cook, stirring, over low heat until smooth.
6 Lift cheesecakes from pan, remove plastic wrap; turn, top-side up, onto plates. Drizzle with chocolate sauce.

prep + cook time 18 minutes
(+ standing & refrigeration) **makes** 6
nutritional count per serving 42.6g total fat
(27.5g saturated fat); 653 cal; 48.9g carbohydrate;
10.2g protein; 2.2g fiber

serving suggestion Serve with vanilla ice cream.

crème brûlée praline tarts

1⅓ cups cream
⅓ cup milk
1 vanilla bean
4 egg yolks
¼ cup superfine sugar

PASTRY
1¼ cups plain (all-purpose) flour
¼ cup superfine sugar
4½ ounces cold butter, chopped coarsely
1 egg yolk

PRALINE
¼ cup superfine sugar
2 tablespoons water
1 tablespoon roasted hazelnuts
2 tablespoons unsalted roasted pistachios

1 Make pastry.
2 Grease six-hole (¾-cup) texas muffin pan. Cut six 4½-inch rounds from pastry. Press rounds into muffin holes; prick bases all over with fork. Refrigerate 30 minutes.
3 Preheat oven to 315°F.
4 Combine cream and milk in small saucepan. Split vanilla bean in half lengthwise; scrape seeds into pan (reserve pod for another use). Bring to a boil. Beat egg yolks and sugar in small bowl with electric mixer until thick and creamy. Gradually whisk hot cream mixture into egg mixture. Pour warm custard into pastry cases.
5 Bake about 30 minutes or until set; cool 15 minutes. Refrigerate 1 hour.
6 Meanwhile, make praline.
7 Preheat grill. Remove tarts from pan; place on oven tray. Sprinkle custard with praline; grill until praline caramelizes. Serve immediately.

PASTRY Process flour, sugar and butter until coarse. Add egg yolk; process until combined. Knead on floured surface until smooth. Roll pastry between sheets of parchment paper to ⅛-inch thickness. Refrigerate 15 minutes.

PRALINE Combine sugar and the water in small saucepan; stir over heat until sugar dissolves. Boil, uncovered, without stirring, about 8 minutes or until golden in color. Place nuts, in single layer, on greased oven tray. Pour toffee over nuts; stand about 15 minutes or until set. Break toffee into large pieces; process until chopped finely.

prep + cook time 1 hour 15 minutes (+ refrigeration, standing and cooling time) makes 6
nutritional count per serving 49.8g total fat (29.1g saturated fat); 694 cal; 52.8g carbohydrate; 8.7g protein; 1.8g fiber

tip If pastry is too dry, add 2 teaspoons of water with egg yolk.

molten mocha cakes

5½ ounces dark chocolate, chopped coarsely
4½ ounces butter, chopped coarsely
3 teaspoons instant coffee granules
2 eggs
2 egg yolks
⅓ cup superfine sugar
¼ cup plain (all-purpose) flour
2 teaspoons cocoa powder

1 Preheat oven to 400°F. Grease six-hole (¾-cup) texas muffin pan well with softened butter.
2 Stir chocolate, butter and coffee in small saucepan, over low heat, until smooth; cool 10 minutes. Transfer to a large bowl.
3 Beat eggs, egg yolks and sugar in small bowl with electric mixer until thick and creamy. Fold egg mixture and sifted flour into barely warm chocolate mixture.
4 Divide mixture among muffin holes; bake, in oven, 12 minutes.
5 Gently turn puddings onto serving plates, top-side down. Serve immediately, dusted with sifted cocoa powder.

prep + cook time 40 minutes **makes** 6
nutritional count per serving 28.6g total fat (16.7g saturated fat); 406 cal; 32.9g carbohydrate; 5.7g protein; 0.9g fiber

serving suggestion Serve with whipped cream and fresh raspberries.

tip Use a good-quality dark chocolate with 70% cocoa solids.

chocolate orange ricotta tarts

1½ cups ricotta cheese
½ cup superfine sugar
1 egg, beaten lightly
3 ounces finely chopped dark chocolate
⅓ cup finely chopped glacé orange
¼ cup golden raisins
3 sheets butter puff pastry
1 tablespoon milk
1 tablespoon confectioners' sugar

1 Preheat oven to 400°F. Line oven trays with parchment paper.
2 Combine cheese, sugar and egg in medium bowl. Stir in chocolate and fruit.

3 Cut twelve 4½-inch circles from pastry; place circles on trays. Divide ricotta mixture among circles, leaving a 1-inch border. Fold pastry edge up. Brush pastry with milk; bake tarts about 12 minutes or until browned. Cool 5 minutes before dusting with sifted confectioner's sugar.

prep + cook time 35 minutes makes 12
nutritional count per serving 15.7g total fat (9.5g saturated fat); 270 cal; 35g carbohydrate; 6.5g protein; 1.1g fiber

141

little salty caramel meringue pies

12½ ounces canned sweetened
     condensed milk
  1 ounce butter
  ¼ cup golden syrup
  2 teaspoons sea salt flakes
  ¼ cup light cream

PASTRY
  1 cup plain (all-purpose) flour
  ⅓ cup confectioners' sugar
  3 ounces butter, chopped coarsely
  1 egg yolk
  1 tablespoon ice water, approximately

MERINGUE
  4 egg whites
  1 cup superfine sugar

1 Make pastry.
2 Divide pastry into eight portions. Roll one portion at a time between sheets of parchment paper until large enough to line eight 3-inch tart pans. Ease pastry into pans, pressing into bottom and side; trim edges. prick bottom with fork. Place on oven tray; refrigerate 20 minutes.
3 Meanwhile, preheat oven to 350°F.
4 Line pastry with parchment paper, fill with dried beans or rice. Bake 10 minutes; remove paper and beans. Bake about 5 minutes or until browned; cool.
5 Combine condensed milk, butter, syrup and salt in small heavy-based saucepan; stir over medium heat about 12 minutes or until caramel-colored. Stir in cream. Spread filling into pastry.
6 Make meringue.
7 Spoon meringue onto tarts. Bake tarts about 5 minutes or until browned lightly.

PASTRY Process flour, confectioners' sugar and butter until crumbly. Add egg yolk and most of the water; process until ingredients just come together. Knead pastry on floured surface until smooth. Enclose with plastic wrap; refrigerate 30 minutes.

MERINGUE Beat egg whites in small bowl with electric mixer until soft peaks form. Add sugar gradually, beating until dissolved between each addition.

prep + cook time 1 hour (+ refrigeration) makes 8
nutritional count per serving 17.9g total fat (11.4g saturated fat); 525 cal; 85.2g carbohydrate; 9.1g protein; 0.7g fiber

chocolate tartlets

5½ ounces dark chocolate
¼ cup heavy cream
1 tablespoon orange-flavored liqueur
1 egg
2 egg yolks
2 tablespoons superfine sugar

PASTRY
1⅔ cups plain (all-purpose) flour
⅓ cup superfine sugar
5½ ounces cold butter, chopped coarsely
1 egg yolk

1 Make pastry.
2 Grease two 12-hole (2-tablespoons) deep tart pans.
3 Roll pastry between sheets of parchment paper to ⅛-inch thickness; cut out twenty-four 2½-inch rounds. Press rounds into muffin holes; prick bases all over with fork. Refrigerate 30 minutes.
4 Preheat oven to 400°F.
5 Bake pastry 10 minutes. Cool.
6 Reduce temperature to 350°F.
7 Combine chocolate, cream and liqueur in small saucepan; stir over low heat until smooth. Cool 5 minutes.
8 Meanwhile, beat egg, egg yolks and sugar in small bowl with electric mixer until light and fluffy; fold chocolate mixture into egg mixture.
9 Divide filling among pastry. Bake 8 minutes; cool 10 minutes. Refrigerate 1 hour. Serve dusted with a little sifted cocoa powder.

PASTRY Process flour, sugar and butter until coarse. Add egg yolk; process until combined. Knead pastry on floured surface until smooth. Cover; refrigerate 30 minutes.

prep + cook time 45 minutes
(+ refrigeration time) serves 24
nutritional count per serving 8.9g total fat
(5.4g saturated fat); 157 cal; 16.5g carbohydrate;
2.2g protein; 0.5g fiber

tip If pastry is too dry, add 2 teaspoons of water with the egg yolk.

caramel cashew tarts

1 cup roasted unsalted cashews
1 tablespoon cornstarch
¾ cup firmly packed brown sugar
2 tablespoons golden syrup
2 ounces butter, melted
2 eggs
2 tablespoons cream
1 teaspoon vanilla extract

PASTRY
1¼ cups plain (all-purpose) flour
¼ cup superfine sugar
4½ ounces cold butter, chopped coarsely
1 egg yolk
2 teaspoons water

CINNAMON CREAM
10 ounces heavy cream
1 tablespoon confectioners' sugar
1 teaspoon ground cinnamon

1 Make pastry.
2 Grease two 12-hole (⅓-cup) muffin pans. Roll pastry between sheets of parchment paper to ⅛-inch thickness; cut out twenty-four 3¼-inch rounds. Press rounds into pan holes; prick bases all over with fork. Refrigerate 20 minutes.
3 Preheat oven to 400°F.
4 Bake pastry 10 minutes. Cool.
5 Reduce temperature to 315°F.
6 Combine nuts and cornstarch in medium bowl; stir in sugar, syrup, butter, egg, cream and extract. Divide filling among pastry. Bake about 15 minutes; cool. Refrigerate 30 minutes.
7 Meanwhile, beat ingredients for cinnamon cream in small bowl with electric mixer until soft peaks form.
8 Serve tarts with cinnamon cream.

PASTRY Process flour, sugar and butter until coarse. Add egg yolk and the water; process until combined. Knead on floured surface until smooth. Cover; refrigerate 30 minutes.

prep + cook time 45 minutes
(+ refrigeration and cooling) **makes** 4
nutritional count per serving 15.2g total fat
(8.2g saturated fat); 223 cal; 18.6g carbohydrate;
29g protein; 0.7g fiber

tip If pastry is too dry, add 2 teaspoons of water with the egg yolk.

dark chocolate and hazelnut frozen parfait

½ cup heavy cream
½ cup chocolate-hazelnut spread
¼ cup coffee-flavored liqueur
2 eggs
3 egg yolks
⅓ cup superfine sugar
1 cup heavy cream, extra
5 ounces dark chocolate, grated coarsely
⅓ cup finely chopped roasted hazelnuts
3½ ounces dark chocolate, grated coarsely, extra

1 Line six-hole (¾-cup) texas muffin pan with paper cases.
2 Combine cream, chocolate-hazelnut spread and liqueur in small saucepan; stir over low heat until smooth.
3 Beat eggs, egg yolks and sugar in small bowl with electric mixer until thick and creamy; with motor operating, gradually beat warm chocolate mixture into egg mixture. Transfer parfait to large bowl; refrigerate 20 minutes or until mixture thickens slightly.
4 Beat extra cream in small bowl with electric mixer until soft peaks form; fold into parfait with grated chocolate and nuts. Pour mixture into cases. Cover loosely with plastic wrap; freeze overnight.
5 Lift parfaits out of pan; serve immediately, topped with extra grated chocolate.

prep + cook time 30 minutes
(+ refrigeration & freezing time) **makes** 6
nutritional count per serving 52.4g total fat
(26.4g saturated fat); 773 cal; 48.9g carbohydrate;
61.2 protein; 2.2g fiber

tip We used freeform paper liners made by pushing a 6¼-inch square of paper (we used paper about the same thickness as printer paper) into ungreased pan holes, followed by a 6¼-inch square of parchment paper.

variation
white chocolate and macadamia frozen parfaits
Omit chocolate-hazelnut spread and replace with 5½ ounces melted white chocolate. Omit grated dark chocolate. Omit hazelnuts and replace with ⅓ cup finely chopped roasted macadamias. Top parfaits with 3½ ounces coarsely grated white chocolate.

sticky banana puddings with butterscotch sauce

4½ ounces butter, softened
⅔ cup firmly packed brown sugar
2 eggs
1½ cups self-raising flour
1 teaspoon mixed spice
1 cup mashed banana
¼ cup sour cream
¼ cup milk
2 tablespoons brown sugar, extra
1 large banana, sliced thinly

BUTTERSCOTCH SAUCE
½ cup firmly packed brown sugar
⅔ cup cream
1¾ ounces butter

1 Preheat oven to 350°F. Grease eight holes of two six-hole (¾-cup) texas muffin pans.
2 Beat butter and sugar in small bowl with electric mixer until light and fluffy. Beat in eggs, one at a time; transfer mixture to large bowl. Stir in sifted flour and spice, mashed banana, sour cream and milk in two batches.
3 Sprinkle extra sugar in muffin holes; cover bases of muffin holes with sliced banana. Divide cake mixture among pan holes. Bake 30 minutes.
4 Meanwhile, make butterscotch sauce.
5 Turn puddings, top-side down, onto serving plates; serve warm with butterscotch sauce.

BUTTERSCOTCH SAUCE Combine ingredients in small saucepan; stir over heat, without boiling, until sugar dissolves. Simmer, stirring, about 3 minutes or until sauce thickens slightly.

prep + cook time 45 minutes **makes** 8
nutritional count per serving 31.6g total fat (20.1g saturated fat); 575 cal; 65.5g carbohydrate; 6.3g protein; 2.1g fiber

serving suggestion Serve with vanilla ice cream.

tip You need 2 large overripe bananas to get the required amount of mashed banana.

tiramisu

1¼ pounds double unfilled round sponge cake
2 tablespoons instant coffee granules
¼ cup boiling water
⅓ cup coffee-flavored liqueur
1 teaspoon gelatin
1 tablespoon boiling water, extra
¾ cup heavy cream
¼ cup confectioner's sugar
1 teaspoon vanilla extract
1½ cups mascarpone cheese

GANACHE
⅔ cup cream
6 ounces dark chocolate, chopped coarsely

1 Make ganache.
2 Line each hole of a greased six-hole (¾-cup) texas muffin pan with plastic wrap. Divide half the ganache over the base of each muffin hole. Refrigerate 20 minutes.
3 Meanwhile, cut each sponge cake into three slices horizontally. Cut six 3¼-inch rounds from three sponge slices and six 2¾-inch rounds from remaining three sponge slices.
4 Dissolve coffee in the boiling water in small pitcher; stir in liqueur.
5 Sprinkle gelatin over the extra boiling water in another small jug; stir until gelatin dissolves. Cool.
6 Beat cream, sifted confectioners' sugar and extract in small bowl with electric mixer until soft peaks form; beat in gelatin mixture. Transfer mixture to large bowl; fold in cheese.
7 Brush both sides of sponge rounds with coffee mixture. Spread half the cheese mixture into the muffin holes; top with small sponge rounds. Spread remaining cheese mixture over sponge layers; top with larger sponge cake rounds.
8 Spread remaining ganache over sponge layers; refrigerate 3 hours or overnight.
9 Remove tiramisu from pan; turn, top-side down, onto serving plates, remove plastic wrap. Serve dusted with a little sifted cocoa powder.

GANACHE Bring cream to the boil in small saucepan; remove from heat. Add chocolate; stir until smooth.

prep + cook time 40 minutes
(+ refrigeration time) **makes** 6
nutritional count per serving 70.5g total fat
(44.6g saturated fat); 1018 cal; 80.6g carbohydrate;
10.8g protein; 2.1g fiber

serving suggestion Serve accompanied by fresh blueberries.

tip Stand remaining ganache at room temperature so it is a spreadable consistency when topping tiramisu.

caramel pecan pie

½ cup golden syrup
¼ cup firmly packed light brown sugar
2 eggs, beaten lightly
1½ ounces butter, melted
2 tablespoons plain (all-purpose) flour
2 teaspoons vanilla extract
1 cup pecans, toasted, halved

PASTRY
1½ cups plain (all-purpose) flour
2 tablespoons confectioners' sugar
4 ounces cold butter, chopped coarsely
1 egg yolk
2 tablespoons iced water, approximately

1 Make pastry.
2 Roll pastry between sheets of parchment paper until large enough to line 9½-inch round loose-based flan pan. Ease pastry into pan, press into base and side; trim edge. Refrigerate 30 minutes.
3 Preheat oven to 400°F.
4 Place pan on oven tray. Line pastry with parchment paper; fill with dried beans or rice. Bake 10 minutes; remove paper and beans. Bake 10 minutes; cool.
5 Reduce oven to 350°F.
6 Combine syrup, confectioners' sugar, eggs, butter, flour and extract in small bowl; whisk until smooth. Pour mixture into pastry case; top with nuts.
7 Bake pie about 40 minutes or until set; cool.

PASTRY Process flour, icing sugar and butter until crumbly. Add egg yolk and enough of the water to make ingredients just come together. Knead dough on floured surface until smooth. Enclose with plastic wrap; refrigerate 30 minutes.

prep + cook time 1 hour 20 minutes
(+ refrigeration) **serves** 8
nutritional count per serving 31.1g total fat
(13.2g saturated fat); 501 cal; 49g carbohydrate;
7.1g protein; 2.4g fiber

strawberry and lemon curd tart

8 ounces fresh strawberries, quartered
1 tablespoon confectioners' sugar

LEMON CURD
3 eggs
3 egg yolks
1 cup superfine sugar
4 ounces butter, chopped coarsely
½ cup lemon juice

SOUR CREAM PASTRY
1½ cups plain (all-purpose) flour
1 tablespoon superfine sugar
2½ ounces butter, chopped coarsely
⅓ cup sour cream
2 teaspoons iced water, approximately

1 Make lemon curd and sour cream pastry.
2 Preheat oven to 400°F. Grease 9½-inch loose-based flan pan.
3 Roll pastry between sheets of parchment paper until large enough to line pan. Lift pastry into pan, ease into base and side; trim edge. Refrigerate 30 minutes. Bake pastry 25 minutes; cool.
4 Spoon lemon curd into pastry; top with strawberries. Serve dusted with sifted confectioners' sugar.

LEMON CURD Whisk eggs, egg yolks and sugar in medium bowl until combined. Melt butter with juice in small saucepan over low heat; bring to the boil, gradually whisk into egg mixture. Return mixture to pan, whisk over low heat about 10 minutes or until thick; cool. Transfer to small bowl, cover, refrigerate overnight.

SOUR CREAM PASTRY Process flour, sugar and butter until crumbly. Add sour cream and enough of the water to make ingredients just come together. Knead dough on floured surface until smooth. Wrap in plastic; refrigerate 30 minutes.

prep + cook time 55 minutes (+ refrigeration)
serves 10
nutritional count per serving 23.2g total fat (14g saturated fat); 316 cal; 42.4g carbohydrate; 6.2g protein; 1.4g fiber

vanilla custard pie

2 sheets puff pastry
2 tablespoons confectioners' sugar
¼ cup slivered almonds
1 cup superfine sugar
1 cup cornstarch
½ cup custard powder
1¼ cups heavy cream
3½ cups milk
1 vanilla bean
2 ounces butter, chopped coarsely
2 egg yolks

1 Preheat oven to 425°F. Grease 9½-inch round springform pan. Line oven trays with parchment paper.
2 Place pastry sheets on oven trays; brush with a little water. Sprinkle evenly with sifted confectioners' sugar. Sprinkle one pastry sheet with nuts. Bake about 15 minutes or until browned lightly. Gently flatten pastry with egg slice. Cut each sheet into 9½-inch rounds. Place plain sheet in pan.
3 Meanwhile, combine superfine sugar, cornstarch and custard powder in medium saucepan. Combine cream and milk in large mixing bowl. Gradually stir milk mixture into sugar mixture, until smooth.
4 Halve vanilla bean lengthways, scrape seeds into pan; add butter. Bring to the boil, stirring constantly until mixture boils and thickens. Simmer about 3 minutes, strring constantly. Remove from heat; stir in egg yolks. Spread mixture over pastry in tin. Top with remaining round, nut side up. Refrigerate, 2 hours or until firm.
5 Serve dusted with a little extra sifted confectioners' sugar.

prep + cook time 40 minutes (+ refrigeration)
serves 10
nutritional count per serving 29.4g total fat (13.8g saturated fat); 521 cal; 59g carbohydrate; 6.6g protein; 0.7g fiber

baking pans

Baking pans come in a variety of shapes and sizes, and in an increasing array of finishes including aluminum, tin, silicone and non-stick coating. If your tray is made of tin or has a non-stick coating, you should cook for slightly less time, and drop the oven temperature by about 50°F. When using silicone trays, follow the manufacturer's instructions as there may be cooking time and temperature variations.

We prefer to grease trays coated with a non-stick surface, especially if they are scratched. When greasing pans, you can use either softened butter or cooking-oil spray. We favor butter, particularly in sweet recipes.

1. **shallow round-based tart pan** This pan is only available in a frame of 12 holes of 1½-tablespoons capacity each. They have a rounded base and are also known as tartlet pans.

2. **deep flat-based tart pan** A flat-based tart pan that usually has 12 round holes with a capacity of 2 tablespoons each.

3. **muffin pan** Round, flat-based pans with a hole capacity of ⅓-cup. Commonly available in 12-hole, but also sometimes found in 24-hole size.

4. **texas muffin pan** Texas, or giant, muffins are made in these large, flat-based, round pans that are usually sold as 6-hole pans of ¾-cup capacity each.

5. **friand pan** These flat-based, oval pans used to be available as individual pans of ½-cup capacity. They are now sold as 6- or 12-hole (½-cup) pans. If you have individual friand pans, stand them on an oven tray to cook.

6. **mini muffin pan** Mini muffin pans consist of tiny round holes of 1-tablespoon capacity with a flat base. They are available in a frame of 6, 12 or 24 holes.

7. **petite loaf pan** Petite loaf pans are available in a variety of capacity sizes, ranging from ½ cup to 2 cups. They are all rectangular in shape and quite deep. Petite loaf pans can be sold individually, or in a frame of either 8 or 12 holes. In this book, we have used a 8-hole ½-cup capacity pan.

8. **madeleine pan** Used solely for making French madeleine cakes, these are available as 12-hole pans of 1½-tablespoons capacity. Serve cakes top-side down to display the shape of the distinctive shell-like fluting of the molds.

index

A

Apples
 Apple and Blackberry Pies, 132
 Apple and Mixed Berry Filo Pie, 130
 French Apple Quince Tarts, 134
 Spiced Apple Parcels, 131
Argentinean Empanadas, 34
Asian Beef and Eggplant Cups, 35
Asparagus, in Sun-Dried Tomato and
 Asparagus Tart, 103
Avocados
 Guacamole, 54
 Salsa, 84

B

Bacon
 Chicken, Bacon & Blue Cheese Jalousie,
 21
 Creamy Bacon and Fish Pie with Potato
 Topping, 110
 Mushroom and Pancetta
 Quiche, 74
 Pizza Muffins, 57
 Sausage, Egg and Bacon Pies, 71
 Baked Cheesy Polenta with Salsa, 84
Baking pans, 154–155
Baking pastry blind, 9
Baklava Figs, 122
Banana puddings with butterscotch sauce,
 sticky, 147
Bastilla, chicken, 23
Beans and legumes
 Beef and Lentil Pies with Mashed Sweet
 Potato, 32
 Curried Beef and Pea Pie, 70
 Four-Bean Chili Pie with Cornbread
 Crust, 94
 Hummus, 76
 Mexican Beef and Bean Pie, 50–51
 Nachos, 54–55
 Spiced Chorizo and Bean Pies, 65
 Spiced Green Pea and Potato
 Pasties, 96
 Vegetable and Lentil Potato Pie, 81
Beef
 Argentinean Empanadas, 34
 Asian Beef and Eggplant Cups, 35
 Beef and Caramelized Onion Pies, 61
 Beef and Lentil Pies with Mashed
 Sweet Potato, 32
 Beef and Onion Party Pies, 43

Beef Pies with Polenta Tops, 40–41
Beef Shiraz Pies, 36–37
Chili Beef Pies with Cornbread Topping,
 33
Chunky Beef and Mushroom Pies, 30–31
Cottage Pie, 39
Curried Beef and Pea Pie, 70
Individual Beef Wellingtons, 62–63
Meat Pie Scrolls, 48
Mexican Beef and Bean Pie, 50–51
Nachos, 54–55
Yorkshire Puddings with Beef and Red
 Wine Stew, 47
Berries
 Apple and Blackberry Pies, 132
 Apple and Mixed Berry Filo Pie, 130
 Berry and Rhubarb Pies, 132–133
 Gooey Chicken, Brie and Cranberry
 Pies, 14
 Strawberry and Lemon Curd Tart, 151
 White Chocolate and Raspberry Bread
 Puddings, 123
 White Chocolate and Raspberry Trifles,
 121
Blood Orange Meringue Pies, 125
Butter, 7
Butter Chicken Puffs, 15
Butternut squash. See Squash
Butterscotch Sauce, 147

C

Caramel
 Caramel Cashew Tarts, 145
 Caramel Pecan Pie, 150
 Chocolate, Peanut and Caramel
 Cheesecakes, 144
 Little Salty Caramel Meringue Pies,
 142–143
Caramelized Leek and Brie Tartlets, 82
Celery root, old-fashioned lamb and, 69
Cheese
 Baked Cheesy Polenta with Salsa, 84
 Butternut Squash and Goat Cheese
 Lasagna, 93
 Caramelized Leek and Brie Tartlets, 82
 Chicken, Bacon & Blue Cheese Jalousie,
 21
 Chocolate Orange Ricotta Tarts, 141
 Chocolate, Peanut and Caramel
 Cheesecakes, 144
 eggs with. See Eggs
 Feta and Spinach Filo Bundles, 83, 102
 Gooey Chicken, Brie and Cranberry
 Pies, 14
 Nachos, 54–55
 Onion and Smoked Cheddar Tarts, 99
 Parmesan Pastry, 99
 Pizza Muffins, 57

Pumpkin and Feta Muffins, 89
Roasted Pepper and Goat
 Cheese Terrine, 101
Smoked Cod and Cheddar Pie, 107
Spinach and Three Cheese Muffins, 88
Tiramisu, 148–149
Tomato, Feta and Pancetta Frittata, 52–53
Chicken. See Poultry pies
Chocolate
 Chocolate Orange Ricotta Tarts, 141
 Chocolate, Peanut and Caramel
 Cheesecakes, 144
 Chocolate Tartlets, 137
 Dark Chocolate and Hazelnut Frozen
 Parfait, 146
 Ganache, 148
 Molten Mocha Cakes, 140
 Tiramisu, 148–149
 White Chocolate and Raspberry Bread
 Puddings, 123
 White Chocolate and Raspberry Trifles,
 121
 White Chocolate, Lime and Ginger
 Mousse Tarts, 126
Chorizo. See Sausage
Chunky Beef and Mushroom Pies, 30–31
Cilantro Chutney, 68
Cinnamon Cream, 145
Cinnamon Pastry, 128
Citrus
 about: lemon juice in pastry, 7
 Blood Orange Meringue Pies, 125
 Chocolate Orange Ricotta Tarts, 141
 Lemon Curd, 151
 Strawberry and Lemon Curd Tart, 151
 White Chocolate, Lime and Ginger
 Mousse Tarts, 126
Coconut, in Passionfruit Curd and Coconut
 Tarts, 127
Coffee
 Molten Mocha Cakes, 140
 Tiramisu, 148–149
Corn and cornmeal
 Baked Cheesy Polenta with Salsa, 84
 Cajun Chicken and Corn Pies, 24
 Cornbread Topping, 33
 Four-Bean Chili Pie with Cornbread
 Crust, 94
 Polenta Pastry, 50
 Polenta Tops, 40–41
 Soft Polenta, 40
Cottage Pie, 39
Country Chicken and Vegetable Pie, 17
Crab, Fennel, and Herb Quiche, 108–109
Cream, maple, 122
Creamy Bacon and Fish Pie with Potato
 Topping, 110
Crème Brûlée Praline Tarts, 139

Curry
    Butter Chicken Puffs, 15
    Curried Beef and Pea Pie, 70
    Curry Shrimp and Roti Pies, 111
    Lamb Masala Pies with Raita, 49
    Mini Vegetable Curry Pies, 98
    Penang Pork Curry Pies, 75
    Rogan Josh Lamb Pie with
    Cilantro Chutney, 68
    Thai Chicken Curry Pies, 16
    Thai Green Curry Chicken Pies, 26
Custard pie, vanilla, 153

D
Dark Chocolate and Hazelnut
Frozen Parfait, 146
Desserts. *See* Sweet pies and tarts
Dishes, lining with pastry, 9
Docking pastry, 9
Double-Crust Pizza, 87
Duck, in Chinese Duck & Five-Spice Pies,
    10–11

E
Eggplant
    Asian Beef and Eggplant Cups, 35
    Eggplant and Hummus Lamb Tarts,
    76–77
    Moussaka Timbales, 45
Eggs
    about: yolk in pastry, 7
    Crab, Fennel, and Herb Quiche, 108–109
    Goat Cheese and Zucchini Flower
    Quiche, 100
    Huevos Rancheros, 97
    Mushroom and Pancetta Quiche, 74
    Prosciutto and Feta Baked Eggs, 58
    Prosciutto and Roasted Red Pepper
    Quiche, 59
    Quiche Primavera, 95
    Roast Sweet Potato and Spinach Frittata,
    85
    Sausage, Egg and Bacon Pies, 71
    Tomato, Feta and Pancetta
    Frittata, 52–53
Empanadas, Argentinean, 34

F
Fennel Pastry, 28
Figs
    Baklava Figs, 122
    Caramelized Onion, Fig and Prosciutto
    Tarts, 64
Fish. *See* Seafood pies
Flour, 7
Four-Bean Chili Pie with Cornbread Crust,
    94
French Apple Quince Tarts, 134

G
Ganache, 148
Ginger Pastry, in White Chocolate, Lime
    and Ginger Mousse Tarts, 126
Gnocchi pie, chicken mushroom and, 27
Gooey Chicken, Brie and Cranberry Pies,
    14
Greek Shrimp Pies, 106
Guacamole, 54

H
Harissa Yogurt, 72–73
Huevos Rancheros, 97
Hummus, 76

I
Individual Beef Wellingtons, 62–63

K
Kneading pastry, 8

L
Lamb
    Eggplant and Hummus Lamb Tarts, 76–77
    Lamb and Rosemary Pies with Scone
    Topping, 67
    Lamb Masala Pies with Raita, 49
    Moroccan Lamb Party Pies, 78
    Moroccan-Style Lamb Pies with Harissa
    Yogurt, 72–73
    Moussaka Timbales, 45
    Old-Fashioned Lamb and Celery Root
    Pie, 69
    Rogan Josh Lamb Pie with Cilantro
    Chutney, 68
Leeks. *See* Onions and leeks
Lentils. *See* Beans and legumes
Lining dish/pan with pastry, 9

M
Meat pies, 28–79
    Argentinean Empanadas, 34
    Asian Beef and Eggplant Cups, 35
    Beef and Caramelized Onion Pies, 61
    Beef and Lentil Pies with Mashed
    Sweet Potato, 32
    Beef and Onion Party Pies, 43
    Beef Pies with Polenta Tops, 40–41
    Beef Shiraz Pies, 36–37
    Caramelized Onion, Fig and
    Prosciutto Tarts, 64
    Chili Beef Pies with Cornbread Topping,
    33
    Chorizo and Potato Galette with Green
    Olives, 66
    Chunky Beef and Mushroom Pies, 30–31
    Chunky Pork and Fennel Pie, 28–29
    Cottage Pie, 39

Curried Beef and Pea Pie, 70
    Eggplant and Hummus Lamb Tarts,
    76–77
    Individual Beef Wellingtons, 62–63
    Lamb and Rosemary Pies with Scone
    Topping, 67
    Lamb Masala Pies with Raita, 49
    Meat Pie Scrolls, 48
    Mexican Beef and Bean Pie, 50–51
    Moroccan Lamb Party Pies, 78
    Moroccan-Style Lamb Pies with Harissa
    Yogurt, 72–73
    Moussaka Timbales, 45
    Mushroom and Pancetta Quiche, 74
    Nachos, 54–55
    Old-Fashioned Lamb and Celery Root
    Pie, 69
    Penang Pork Curry Pies, 75
    Pizza Muffins, 57
    Pork Sausage and Apple Pie, 60
    Prosciutto and Feta Baked Eggs, 58
    Prosciutto and Roasted Red Pepper
    Quiche, 59
    Rogan Josh Lamb Pie with Cilantro
    Chutney, 68
    Sausage, Egg and Bacon Pies, 71
    Spanish Tortillas, 56
    Spiced Chorizo and Bean Pies, 65
    Tomato, Feta and Pancetta Frittata, 52–53
    Veal and Tomato Pies with Gremolata, 38
    Veal Goulash Pies, 79
    Yorkshire Puddings with Beef and Red
    Wine Stew, 47
Meringue
    Little Salty Caramel Meringue Pies,
    142–143
    Rhubarb Pies with Meringue Topping,
    135
Mexican Beef and Bean Pie, 50–51
Mince pies, whiskey-laced, 128
Mini Vegetable Curry Pies, 98
Molten Mocha Cakes, 140
Moroccan Lamb Party Pies, 78
Moroccan-Style Lamb Pies with Harissa
    Yogurt, 72–73
Moussaka Timbales, 45
Muffins
    Basic Muffin Mix, 57
    Pizza Muffins, 57
    Pumpkin and Feta Muffins, 89
    Spinach and Three Cheese Muffins, 88
Mushrooms
    Chicken and Mushroom Party Pies, 19
    Chicken, Mushroom & Tarragon Pies, 12
    Chicken, Mushroom and Gnocchi Pie, 27
    Chunky Beef and Mushroom Pies, 30–31
    Country Chicken and Vegetable Pie, 17
    Mushroom and Pancetta Quiche, 74

N

Nachos, 54–55
Nuts
Caramel Cashew Tarts, 145
Caramel Pecan Pie, 150
Chocolate, Peanut and Caramel
Cheesecakes, 144
Crème Brûlée Praline Tarts, 139
Dark Chocolate and Hazelnut Frozen
Parfait, 146
Spinach and Walnut Pesto, 101

O

Old-Fashioned Lamb and Celery Root Pie,
69
Olives
Chorizo and Potato Galette with Green
Olives, 66
Olive and Roasted Tomato Tart, 86
Onions and leeks
Beef and Caramelized Onion Pies, 61
Beef and Onion Party Pies, 43
Caramelized Leek and Brie Tartlets, 82
Caramelized Onion, Fig and
Prosciutto Tarts, 64
Chicken and Leek Strudel, 25
Onion and Smoked Cheddar Tarts, 99
Oranges. See Citrus

P

Pancetta. See Bacon
Pans, baking, 154–155
Pans, lining with pastry, 9
Parmesan Pastry, 99
Party pies
Beef and Onion Party Pies, 43
Chicken and Mushroom Party Pies, 19
Moroccan Lamb Party Pies, 78
Passionfruit Curd and Coconut Tarts, 127
Pasta
Butternut Squash and Goat Cheese
Lasagna, 93
Chicken, Mushroom and Gnocchi Pie, 27
Tuna, Pasta and Chargrilled Vegetable
Pie, 117
Pastry
about, 6–9; baking blind, 9; butter in, 7;
docking, 9; egg yolk in, 7; flour in, 7;
ingredients, 7; kneading, 8; lemon juice
in, 7; lining dish/pan with, 9; resting, 8;
rolling, 8; water in, 7
Butternut Squash and Goat Cheese
Lasagna, 93
Cinnamon Pastry, 128
Fennel Pastry, 28
Ginger Pastry, 126
Parmesan Pastry, 99
Polenta Pastry, 50

Shortcrust Pastry, 6
Sour Cream Pastry, 13, 36, 151
Spicy Pastry, 90
Sweet Shortcrust Pastry (variation), 6
Tarragon Pastry, 12
Pear and Cinnamon Sugar Lattice Pies, 129
Peas. See Beans and legumes
Penang Pork Curry Pies, 75
Peppers
Prosciutto and Roasted Red Pepper
Quiche, 59
Roasted Pepper and Goat Cheese
Terrine, 101
Pesto, spinach and walnut, 101
Pizza
Double-Crust Pizza, 87
Pizza Dough, 87
Pizza Muffins, 57
Polenta. See Corn and cornmeal
Pork. See also Bacon; Prosciutto; Sausage
Chunky Pork and Fennel Pie, 28–29
Penang Pork Curry Pies, 75
Tomato, Feta and Pancetta Frittata, 52–53
Potatoes
Chorizo and Potato Galette with Green
Olives, 66
Cottage Pie, 39
Country Chicken and Vegetable Pie, 17
Creamy Bacon and Fish Pie with Potato
Topping, 110
Fish Pies with Potato Topping, 112–113
Salmon and Potato Soufflés, 118
Spiced Green Pea and Potato Pasties, 96
Vegetable and Lentil Potato Pie, 81
Poultry pies, 10–27
Butter Chicken Puffs, 15
Cajun Chicken and Corn Pies, 24
Chicken and Leek Strudel, 25
Chicken and Mushroom Party Pies, 19
Chicken, Bacon & Blue Cheese Jalousie,
21
Chicken Bastilla, 23
Chicken, Fennel and Celery Pie, 13
Chicken, Mushroom & Tarragon Pies, 12
Chicken, Mushroom and Gnocchi Pie, 27
Chinese Duck & Five-Spice Pies, 10–11
Country Chicken and Vegetable Pie, 17
Gooey Chicken, Brie and Cranberry
Pies, 14
Smoky Paprika Chicken Tart, 22
Spanish Chicken Pie, 20
Thai Chicken Curry Pies, 16
Thai Green Curry Chicken Pies, 26
Vietnamese Chicken Wonton Cups, 18
Prosciutto
Caramelized Onion, Fig and
Prosciutto Tarts, 64
Prosciutto and Feta Baked Eggs, 58

Prosciutto and Roasted Red Pepper
Quiche, 59
Pumpkin and Feta Muffins, 89

Q

Quiches
Crab, Fennel, and Herb Quiche, 108–109
Goat Cheese and Zucchini Flower
Quiche, 100
Mushroom and Pancetta Quiche, 74
Prosciutto and Roasted Red Pepper
Quiche, 59
Quiche Primavera, 95
Quince, in French Apple Quince Tarts, 134

R

Raisins, in Whiskey-Laced Mince Pies, 128
Raita, 49
Resting pastry, 8
Rhubarb
Berry and Rhubarb Pies, 132–133
Rhubarb Pies with Meringue Topping, 135
Roasted Garlicky Squash and Sage Pies,
90–91
Roasted Pepper and Goat Cheese Terrine,
101
Roast Sweet Potato and Spinach Frittata, 85
Rogan Josh Lamb Pie with Cilantro Chutney,
68
Rolling pastry, 8
Roti, in Curry Shrimp and Roti Pies, 111

S

Salmon
Salmon and Potato Soufflés, 118
Salmon Coulibiac, 116
Smoked Salmon Vol-au-Vents, 114
Salty Caramel Meringue Pies, 142–143
Sauces and toppings, sweet. See also
Meringue
Butterscotch Sauce, 147
Cinnamon Cream, 145
Ganache, 148
Maple Cream, 122
Sauces, spreads, and dips
Cilantro Chutney, 68
Guacamole, 54
Harissa Yogurt, 72–73
Hummus, 76
Raita, 49
Salsa, 84
Spinach and Walnut Pesto, 101
Tomato Sauce, 30
Sausage
Chorizo and Potato Galette with Green
Olives, 66
Pork Sausage and Apple Pie, 60
Sausage, Egg and Bacon Pies, 71

Spanish Tortillas, 56
Spiced Chorizo and Bean Pies, 65
Scallop pies, Thai-flavored, 115
Scone Topping, 67
Scrolls, meat pie, 48
Seafood pies, 104–119
    Crab, Fennel, and Herb Quiche, 108–109
    Creamy Bacon and Fish Pie with Potato
        Topping, 110
    Curry Shrimp and Roti Pies, 111
    Fish Chowder Pies, 119
    Fish Pies with Potato Topping, 112–113
    Greek Shrimp Pies, 106
    Salmon and Potato Soufflés, 118
    Salmon Coulibiac, 116
    Smoked Cod and Cheddar Pie, 107
    Smoked Salmon Vol-au-Vents, 114
    Thai-Flavored Scallop Pies, 115
    Tomato and Saffron Fish Pies, 105
    Tuna, Pasta and Chargrilled
        Vegetable Pie, 117
Shrimp
    Curry Shrimp and Roti Pies, 111
    Greek Shrimp Pies, 106
Smoked Cod and Cheddar Pie, 107
Smoked Salmon Vol-au-Vents, 114
Smoky Paprika Chicken Tart, 22
Sour Cream Pastry, 13, 36, 151
Spanish Chicken Pie, 20
Spanish Tortillas, 56
Spiced Apple Parcels, 131
Spiced Chorizo and Bean Pies, 65
Spiced Green Pea and Potato Pasties, 96
Spicy Pastry, 90
Spinach
    Feta and Spinach Filo Bundles, 83, 102
    Roast Sweet Potato and Spinach Frittata,
        85
    Spinach and Three Cheese Muffins, 88
    Spinach and Walnut Pesto, 101
Squash
    Butternut Squash and Goat Cheese
        Lasagna, 93
    Goat Cheese and Zucchini Flower
        Quiche, 100
    Roasted Garlicky Squash and Sage Pies,
        90–91
Sticky Banana Puddings with Butterscotch
    Sauce, 147
Strawberry and Lemon Curd Tart, 151
Strudel, chicken and leek, 25
Sun-Dried Tomato and Asparagus Tart,
    103
Sweet pies and tarts, 120–153. See also
    Sauces and toppings, sweet
    Apple and Blackberry Pies, 132
    Apple and Mixed Berry Filo Pie, 130
    Baklava Figs, 122

Berry and Rhubarb Pies, 132–133
Blood Orange Meringue Pies, 125
Caramel Cashew Tarts, 145
Caramel Pecan Pie, 150
Chocolate Orange Ricotta Tarts, 141
Chocolate, Peanut and Caramel
    Cheesecakes, 144
Chocolate Tartlets, 137
Crème Brûlée Praline Tarts, 139
Dark Chocolate and Hazelnut Frozen
    Parfait, 146
French Apple Quince Tarts, 134
Little Salty Caramel Meringue Pies,
    142–143
Molten Mocha Cakes, 140
Passionfruit Curd and Coconut Tarts, 127
Pear and Cinnamon Sugar Lattice Pies,
    129
Rhubarb Pies with Meringue Topping, 135
Spiced Apple Parcels, 131
Sticky Banana Puddings with
    Butterscotch Sauce, 147
Strawberry and Lemon Curd Tart, 151
Tiramisu, 148–149
Vanilla Custard Pie, 153
Whiskey-Laced Mince Pies, 128
White Chocolate and Raspberry Bread
    Puddings, 123
White Chocolate and Raspberry Trifles,
    121
White Chocolate, Lime and Ginger
    Mousse Tarts, 126
Sweet potatoes
    Beef and Lentil Pies with Mashed Sweet
        Potato, 32
    Roast Sweet Potato and Spinach Frittata,
        85
    Vegetable and Lentil Potato Pie, 81

T
Tarragon Pastry, 12
Thai Chicken Curry Pies, 16
Thai-Flavored Scallop Pies, 115
Thai Green Curry Chicken Pies, 26
Tiramisu, 148–149
Tomatoes
    Olive and Roasted Tomato Tart, 86
    sauces with. See Sauces, spreads, and
        dips
    Sun-Dried Tomato and Asparagus Tart,
        103
    Tomato and Saffron Fish Pies, 105
    Tomato, Feta and Pancetta Frittata,
        52–53
    Veal and Tomato Pies with Gremolata,
        38
Tuna, Pasta and Chargrilled Vegetable Pie,
    117

V
Vanilla Custard Pie, 153
Veal
    Veal and Tomato Pies with Gremolata, 38
    Veal Goulash Pies, 79
Veal and Tomato Pies with Gremolata, 38
Vegetable pies, 80–103
    Baked Cheesy Polenta with Salsa, 84
    Butternut Squash and Goat Cheese
        Lasagna, 93
    Caramelized Leek and Brie Tartlets, 82
    Country Chicken and Vegetable Pie, 17
    Double-Crust Pizza, 87
    Feta and Spinach Filo Bundles, 83, 102
    Four-Bean Chili Pie with Cornbread
        Crust, 94
    Goat Cheese and Zucchini Flower
        Quiche, 100
    Huevos Rancheros, 97
    Mini Vegetable Curry Pies, 98
    Olive and Roasted Tomato Tart, 86
    Onion and Smoked Cheddar Tarts, 99
    Pumpkin and Feta Muffins, 89
    Quiche Primavera, 95
    Roasted Garlicky Squash and Sage Pies,
        90–91
    Roasted Pepper and Goat Cheese
        Terrine, 101
    Roast Sweet Potato and Spinach Frittata,
        85
    Spiced Green Pea and Potato Pasties, 96
    Spinach and Three Cheese Muffins, 88
    Sun-Dried Tomato and Asparagus Tart,
        103
    Tuna, Pasta and Chargrilled Vegetable
        Pie, 117
    Vegetable and Lentil Potato Pie, 81
Vietnamese Chicken Wonton Cups, 18
Vol-au-vents, smoked, 114

W
Whiskey-Laced Mince Pies, 128
White chocolate. See Chocolate
Wonton cups, Vietnamese chicken, 18

Y
Yogurt
    Harissa Yogurt, 72–73
    Raita, 49
Yorkshire Puddings with Beef and Red
    Wine Stew, 47

Z
Zucchini. See Squash

STERLING
New York

An Imprint of Sterling Publishing
387 Park Avenue South
New York, NY 10016

ISBN 978-1-4549-1316-0

Distributed in Canada by Sterling Publishing
c/o Canadian Manda Group, 165 Dufferin Street
Toronto, Ontario, Canada M6K 3H6

For information about custom editions, special sales, and premium and corporate purchases,
please contact Sterling Special Sales at 800-805-5489 or specialsales@sterlingpublishing.com.

Manufactured in China

2 4 6 8 10 9 7 5 3 1

www.sterlingpublishing.com